# JC STOTT

*Pastor, leader and friend*

# JOHN STOTT

*Pastor, leader and friend*

## CHRIS WRIGHT · LINDSAY BROWN *et al*

EXPANDED AND UPDATED

In association with

Evangelical Fellowship in
the Anglican Communion

First published as a Didasko File, 2012
Expanded and updated edition published by Dictum / EFAC 2020

Dictum Press, Oxford, UK
*www.dictumpress.com*

Photographs used by kind permission
Snowy owl: Lion Hudson Ltd
All Souls Church: All Souls collection

Design by Chris Gander

Printed in the UK

*With thankfulness for the joint legacy
of John Stott and his lifetime Secretary,
Frances Whitehead. 'One of the greatest
partnerships in church history.'*

# CONTENTS

# FROM THE EDITOR

The original idea for this collection grew out of a conversation with Chris Wright and Doug Birdsall in October 2011, three months after John Stott died, and a list of contributors quickly came together. All writers gladly gave priority to their pieces, so voices were captured while memories were still vivid, and the first edition appeared shortly afterwards, in January 2012.

From the start we knew it would be impossible to contract such a rich and multi-faceted life as that of John Stott into this format. But we trust, for all its inadequacy, that these pages will open up his story to more people, in English and in translation. It complements *John Stott: A portrait by his friends*, the *Festschrift* brought together by Chris Wright to mark John's 90th birthday. Perhaps in due course they will come to be regarded as companion volumes.

Readers will find a strikingly constant note throughout these pages, a tribute in itself. The seminal influence over decades of works like *Basic Christianity*, *Your Mind Matters*, *Issues Facing Christians Today* and *The Cross of Christ* comes through clearly. Repetition of titles of books, and of references to the same events, has been left intact to retain the integrity of each contribution. A number of writers refer to 'Uncle John'. He liked to be called this as, in his words, 'it implies relationship'.

Several doctorates on John Stott's life and ministry have already been completed and more will come. Few people have developed so wide an intellectual reach, or made such an extensive contribution through writing and editing. We're grateful to Timothy Dudley-Smith for his work in compiling a bibliography of all Stott's writing up to 1995.[1]

In a personal conversation in 2008, John expressed his hope that the 1978 Lausanne Movement *Willowbank Report on Gospel and Culture* would not be forgotten. Its principles of engagement remain unchanged, regardless of the speed of light at which culture reinvents itself, and I am glad to commend this report, on his behalf, as a starting point for all future exploration of this area.[2]

I'm grateful to Bishop Michael Nazir-Ali for his Foreword to this edition. I'm also grateful to all the contributors for sharing their stories, insights, and perspectives. Some speak for continents, others for movements or ministries; each writer also speaks from a sense of personal appreciation.

We send this collection on its way with the hope and prayer that it will bring readers new insights into

---

1. *John Stott: A comprehensive bibliography*, Timothy Dudley-Smith (IVP-UK, 1995; IVP-US, 1996).

2. A thorough work by some of the best evangelical thinkers of the day, published in *Making Christ Known: Historic Mission Documents from The Lausanne Movement 1974-1989* with a valuable Introduction, Paternoster, 1996. Or available at lausanne.org as *Occasional Paper 2* (January 1978). See also *Down to Earth: Studies in Christianity and Culture*. Ed: John Stott and Robert Coote (Hodder and Stoughton, 1981).

the life of John Stott and the ministries founded and fostered by him. The links which grew between those ministries will be a study in itself for future church historians, each endeavour remaining distinct as well as inter-connected.

'Remember your leaders, who spoke the word of God to you. Consider the outcome of their way of life and imitate their faith.' (Hebrews 13:7)

**Julia E M Cameron**
*Oxford, UK*

**A technical note:**

(i) Book titles of John Stott's works have a footnote only when a page number is cited, or if a note will support the narrative thread. A full list of his books is included on p123, with details of the first publisher for each.

(ii) Rules governing the use of upper/lower case for the noun 'church' have proved less than straightforward in places. We have therefore used lower case throughout.

(iii) The term secretary starts with upper case when referring to John Stott's Secretary, as it was Frances Whitehead's job title.

(iv) We have followed the NIV (1984, 2011) in using lower case for gospel, and for the word of God, unless the reference is to Christ.

(v) The terms 'Majority World' and 'Global South' are used interchangeably. They have been left in the form preferred by the writer.

# GLOSSARY OF INITIALS

**CBE** Commander of the Order of the British Empire

**CICCU** Cambridge Inter-Collegiate Christian Union, made up of Christian Union groups in each of the Cambridge colleges.

**EFAC** Evangelical Fellowship in the Anglican Communion, founded by John Stott in 1961. The Church of England Evangelical Council (CEEC), founded by Stott in 1960, is its English member.

**ELT** Evangelical Literature Trust, founded by John Stott in 1971 to provide books for the church in the Majority World. It is now called Langham Literature.

**GAFCON** Global Anglican Future Conference, founded in 2008 to unite Anglicans of an orthodox persuasion.

**GBU** Groupes Bibliques Universitaires, the name used by IFES movements in the Francophone world.

**LICC** London Institute for Contemporary Christianity seeks to equip Christians with a biblical worldview (i) of their professions, and (ii) of cultural and political trends.

**IVP-UK** Inter Varsity Press, founded as the publishing arm of Inter Varsity Fellowship, now UCCF. IVP-US Intervarsity Press, founded as the publishing arm of US Intervarsity.

**IFES** International Fellowship of Evangelical Students serves national student movements (like UCCF UK / Intervarsity USA) in over 160 nations. New movements are pioneered as political and religious situations allow.

**NIFES** Nigerian Fellowship of Evangelical Students, one of the largest IFES national movements.

**UCCF** Universities and Colleges Christian Fellowship (founded as the Inter-Varsity Fellowship) serves the student Christian Unions across England, Scotland and Wales. (Ireland was included until 1999, when a separate movement was established.)

# TIMELINE OF JOHN STOTT'S LIFE AND MINISTRY

**1921** Born in London on 27 April. Baptized in Marylebone Parish Church

**1927-1929** King Arthur's School, Kensington

**1929 -1935** Oakley Hall School, Cirencester

**1935-1940** Rugby School

**1938** Converted to Christ through the influence of schoolfriend John Bridger and Scripture Union public schools evangelist E J H Nash, known as 'Bash'

**1940-1943** Trinity College, Cambridge

**1943-1945** Ridley Hall, Cambridge

**1945-1950** Curate, All Souls Church, Langham Place, London

**1950-1975** Rector, All Souls Langham Place, then Rector Emeritus

**1951** Shaped new direction of World Evangelical Fellowship

**1956** Appointed Frances Whitehead as Secretary

**1959 – 1991** Chaplain to the Queen, then Extra Chaplain to the Queen

**1960** Founder, Church of England Evangelical Council (CEEC); Co-founder with J I Packer, Latimer House.

**1961** Founder, Evangelical Fellowship in the Anglican Communion (EFAC)

**1967** Initiated National Evangelical Anglican Congress (NEAC) and Evangelical Fellowship in the Church in Wales (EFCW)

**1969** Founded Langham Trust

**1971** Founded Evangelical Literature Trust

**1974** Lausanne Congress on World Evangelization. Chief Architect, *The Lausanne Covenant*

**1975** Established first London Lectures in Contemporary Christianity

**1979 -2011** Vice-President, then lifelong Ambassador-at-Large, IFES

**1982** Founded the London Institute for Contemporary Christianity (LICC)

**1983** Received Lambeth DD

**1983-1997** President of Tearfund

**1989** Second Lausanne Congress on World Evangelization. Chief Architect, *Manila Manifesto*

**1991** Two *Festschriften* published for 70th birthday[3]

**2001** Celebration of 80th birthday. Launch of appeal for The Hookses expansion.

**2002** Founded Langham Partnership International

**2004** Made lifelong Honorary Chairman, Lausanne Movement

**2005** (April) Included in *TIME* magazine's list of '100 most influential people'

**2006** Awarded CBE in Queen's New Year's Honours list

**2006** Final international trip, to China and Hong Kong

**2007** Moved into the College of St Barnabas

**2008** Final trip to The Hookses

**2010** *The Radical Disciple* published 'to say goodbye' to his readers

**2011** *Festschrift* to mark 90th birthday[4]

**2011** Died 27 July in St Barnabas College, Lingfield, Surrey

**2011** *The Times, Independent, Guardian, Telegraph* carried obituaries on 29 July. Tributes featured on the BBC, and appeared in media around the world; thanksgiving services took place on all continents; photos and stories were added to a memorial website.

**2011** Funeral, 8 August at All Souls, Langham Place, led by the Revd Hugh Palmer, Rector of All Souls. Caroline Bowerman, John Stott's niece, gave the family tribute

**2011** Service for interment of ashes, 4 September at St James's, Dale, Pembrokeshire, led by the Revd Bill Lewis

**2011** Papers archived in Lambeth Palace Library, London

**2012** Memorial service, 13 January in St Paul's Cathedral, London, led by Bishop Michael Baughen, former Rector of All Souls, and 39th Bishop of Chester

---

3. *AD 2000 and Beyond: A mission agenda*, Eds: Vinay Samuel and Chris Sugden (Regnum); *The Gospel in the Modern World*, Eds Martyn Eden and David F Wells (IVP).

4. *John Stott: A Portrait by his Friends* Ed Chris Wright (IVP).

# FOREWORD

I welcome this expanded collection of pieces on John Stott, written largely by those who knew him well. It is the right time to assess again the life, thought and legacy of this remarkable Christian.

I first met John fifty years ago, when I was a young ordinand, and he already a senior leader, pastor and evangelist. After that meeting, we never lost touch. He graciously gave time to me, and Valerie, my wife, at his flat in London, or in our own home; and he maintained contact, as he did with so many, through his wise, patient and meticulous correspondence, all in long hand!

We knew that whenever there was a crisis – political, social, ecclesiastical or personal - John was always ready to listen and to help. He was a rock for us during two periods of serious persecution, one a long way from him in Pakistan, and the other in the United Kingdom. We shall forever be grateful to him for that, and for much else.

One of the contributions of the Anglican tradition has been serious study of the Bible and the background to its different books: what the writers intended the text to mean; how the church has understood and interpreted it; and how we should seek to apply it to ourselves and to the world around us. John was one of the foremost exemplars of this approach and, moreover, it was he who taught me how to use the Bible in preaching.

The Anglican tradition has been committed to expository preaching, which should never become stale for preacher or congregation. More, Anglicanism also expresses how the Bible is to be used thematically for the seasons of the Church's year, to address particular issues,[5] and how it should be used on special occasions in the life of a community or the nation. John Stott's 'double listening', of attending to God's Word, and to the world around us, is surely required if the church is to remain faithful to Scripture, united in the apostolic faith, and engaged with contemporary issues.

John was not just an evangelical who happened to be Anglican. As Bishop Timothy Dudley-Smith explains, he had drunk deeply from the Anglican tradition, and this was one of the reasons why he was so widely acclaimed in the Anglican world. He did not hesitate to discuss and debate with Anglicans who were very different from himself, as his debate with David Edwards has shown.[6] I remember accompanying him on one occasion when he was preaching at Southwark Cathedral, that great shrine to liberal Anglicanism! His

---

5. See John Stott's own use of the church's year in *Through the year with John Stott* (Monarch, 2020 edition. Foreword by Chris Wright).

6. See *Essentials: A liberal - evangelical dialogue* by John Stott and David L Edwards (Hodder, 1988). See also footnote 19.

sermon was gracious, reasoned and firmly biblical. Even there, it was well received.

His disagreement with Dr Martyn Lloyd-Jones at the National Assembly of Evangelicals in 1966 about whether evangelicals should leave their denominations and establish an evangelical church is well known.[7] He urged younger evangelicals to stay in the Church of England because it was 'comprehensive'. I asked him about this just before he moved into St Barnabas' Clergy Home in 2007 and after the ructions in the Anglican Communion on human sexuality. His measured reply over a kebab lunch can be summed up in two words: he said that he had always believed in 'principled comprehensiveness'. That is to say, orthodox Anglicans could continue to belong to their denomination as long as there was a consensus about essentials, but not if those essentials were widely repudiated, whether in the formularies or in practice.

His Anglican allegiance did not, of course, mean isolationism. He was ready to work with Christians from other traditions. His involvement both with the World Evangelical Fellowship (now the World Evangelical Alliance) and with the World Council of Churches is noted within these pages. We see here, too, both his leadership in the Lausanne Movement, from its very inception, which required co-operation with Christians from very different backgrounds, and his immersion in

---

7. For a detailed account, see *John Stott: A Global Ministry* by Timothy Dudley-Smith (IVP authorized biography Vol 2) pp 65-71.

IFES.[8] More surprising for some was the lead he took in the Evangelical - Roman Catholic Dialogue on Mission, and his co-editing, with Monsignor Basil Meeking, of its final report which does not pretend to be an agreed statement, with some significant areas of divergence as well as convergence and agreement.[9]

John's faith was lively and warm but he was no pietist, if by that is meant 'all heart and no head'. His published works, whether Bible commentaries, books on discipleship or books tackling current issues, all breathe a reasoned presentation of the gospel so that there remains no excuse for rejecting it. For him faith rested on a knowledge of God's character as revealed primarily in Jesus Christ, and in the salvation history of the biblical narrative; but also in Creation and in the testimony of our own hearts.  Such an approach was welcomed by thoughtful students in the many university missions of which his addresses formed a focal point.

He was committed to an effective Christian presence in 'secular' universities and was somewhat wary of Christian universities because of the danger of creating a ghetto mentality among Christians. He did not live to see the day when free speech in the 'secular'

8. Through John Stott's deep links in IFES and in Lausanne, it soon became impossible to pull apart these ministries and the ministries he founded (which were to become Langham Partnership). That is, staff of one are board members of another.

9. *The Evangelical-Roman Catholic Dialogue on Mission* 1977-1984. Eds: B Meeking and J R W Stott (Paternoster and Eerdmans, 1986).

universities would come under threat, and where Christian witness would be silenced and excluded.

The assumptions of freedom and a fair hearing now no longer hold, and it has become difficult, if not impossible, to teach and learn from a biblical perspective, and to address controversial issues in faithfulness to the historic teaching of the Church. Would he have become more sympathetic, I wonder, to the idea of a Christian university which models what a university should be, in terms of an holistic approach to knowledge which is accessible to all, while firmly grounded in a Christian worldview? Such a university would aim for excellence, especially in areas which cannot now be easily addressed in institutions with a secular worldview. This would not mean, of course, that all Christians would choose to go to a Christian institution. Most would still go to secular ones and what John has to say about being a Christian in such settings is even more important now than it was in the past.

At the beginning of the eighteenth century Evangelical Revival (which extended into the early nineteenth century), evangelicals were socially very active whether in the campaign against the slave trade or slavery itself, or in campaigns to improve the lot of working men, women and children in the UK and more widely in the emerging British Empire. According to David Bebbington, eminent historian of evangelicalism in Britain, the advent and growing influence of premillennialism[10] cut the nerve of social involvement. What was the point of improving things if the world faced inevitable doom?[11]

It was not until the 1960s and 1970s that evangelicals began to recover their awareness of social responsibility, and its corollary, social justice. As we see through the Congress on World Evangelization in 1974 (pp54-67), John was able to articulate the growing consensus amongst evangelicals that evangelism and social responsibility, whilst distinct from one another, were integrally related in the mission of the church. He chaired the small drafting group that produced the *Lausanne Covenant*, emanating from that gathering, which was to become so influential in the revival of holistic mission amongst evangelicals. At a subsequent conference at Grand Rapids, Michigan (1982), evangelism and social responsibility were described as being like the two blades of a pair of scissors or the two wings of a bird.[12] Such a statement was entirely consistent with the way in which John's thought was moving. In due course, it would find mature expression in his landmark book *Issues Facing Christians Today*.

---

10. The belief that the world is under imminent sentence of death and that Christ will return soon to inaugurate his millennial reign.

11. See *Evangelicalism in Modern Britain* by David W Bebbington (Unwin Hayman, 1989), pp263ff.

12. 'Evangelism and Social Responsibility: An evangelical commitment'. For the full statement with a Foreword by John Stott, as Chair of the Drafting Committee, see *Making Christ Known*, pp 165-209. Also available at *lausanne.org* as *Lausanne Occasional Paper 21*.

As we are about to discover, John had a privileged life and spent most of it in the environs of 'posh' London. But even here, from his days as curate onwards, it is noteworthy that he gave careful attention to the poorer parts of the All Souls Parish.[13] Instead of using his privilege to advance his own interests, or to increase his comfort, he placed it wholly at the disposal of the Church, at first in the United Kingdom and then, increasingly, in its mission worldwide.

Most of those reading this book will also be blessed with education, skills and knowledge. You may have a position of leadership in church or society or have been entrusted with significant wealth. In our reading of the pages that follow, we will be challenged about how we are using the gifts and resources which the Lord has given us for the sake of the gospel and the Kingdom of God which it announces. Without any doubt, we can take John Stott as our example and guide in sacrificial and creative service of God's plan for his world.

**+Michael Nazir-Ali**

*Bishop Michael Nazir-Ali, 106th Bishop of Rochester (1994-2009) is Director of the Oxford Centre for Training, Research, Advocacy and Dialogue (OXTRAD), a Trustee of GAFCON UK, and a member of the GAFCON International Council.*

13. For more see *John Stott: The Making of a Leader* by Timothy Dudley-Smith (IVP authorized biography Vol 1) pp 270-272. Also *John Stott: A Global Ministry*, Vol 2, pp 20, 23-24, 49-50.

# PART I

# JOHN STOTT THE MAN

# JOHN R W STOTT

## A biographical sketch

John Robert Walmsley Stott, fourth child and only son of Sir Arnold Stott, Extra Physician to the Royal Household, and Lady (Lily) Stott, was born in London on 27 April 1921; he died on the afternoon of 27 July 2011, in the College of St Barnabas, a home for retired clergy, in Surrey, England. As a small child, John joined the Sunday School at All Souls, Langham Place, and he was to serve its congregation and parish as assistant curate, Rector and Rector Emeritus. His global ministry remained anchored here throughout his life.

John Stott's childhood was spent in Harley Street and he was to live within a few minutes' walk of All Souls[14] for over eighty-five years. He was a Chaplain to the Queen, honoured with the CBE, and named as one of the '100 most influential people in the world' by *TIME* magazine.[15]

He wore privilege lightly. He turned his Rectory into what was nicknamed the 'Wreckage', sharing it with others and welcoming many guests.[16] From 1970-2007

---

14. Situated between Oxford Circus and Regents Park.

15. 2005, April issue.

16. This combined the first half of Rectory with the second half of Vicarage, adding a dash of humour.

he lived in a modest two-roomed flat, built above the garage behind the Rectory. John Stott advocated the simple lifestyle, and he practised it.

John Stott had a deep appreciation of the natural world, and a rather British sense of humour, which never left him. From early childhood, his father took him on nature walks, teaching him to watch and to listen. At the same time, his nanny was taking him to the Sunday School at All Souls, where he was armed with plastic daggers and a toy gun to terrify the girls. (He reputedly spent more time outside the classroom than inside.) In his writing retreat at The Hookses, on the Pembrokeshire coast, he kept his binoculars on his desk, which overlooked the bay with its rich birdlife. A copy of Saki's short stories sat on the bookshelves to his right. He would read Saki to his guests, often laughing so much at the stories that he could barely continue to read them![17] The ability to make people laugh was, he remarked, when aged almost 87, 'a forgotten charisma'.

The calling, gifting, *métier*, of this unusually-able man was unique. He had no peer and, as Archbishop Peter Jensen said in the Thanksgiving service in Sydney Cathedral, we should not look for a successor. At the Thanksgiving service in Vancouver, Prof J I Packer paid

---

17. His favourite story was 'The Lumber Room' about a boy who was punished by his aunt for claiming there was a frog in his bread-and-milk. (He had put it there himself, so he spoke with authority on the matter.) His revenge on his aunt was very sweet...

tribute to 'a fifteen talent man'. He described himself as a pastor, a leader and a friend.

As a humble disciple of Christ, he would greet the three Persons of the Trinity in turn each morning, seeking genuinely to live as a son of his heavenly Father, as a sinner saved by grace, and in the power of the Holy Spirit, his advocate and counsellor.

In an interview in 2007 with Brian Draper, to mark the 25th anniversary of LICC, he was asked how he would most like to be remembered. He was by this stage speaking slowly, and occasionally faltering, but there was no hesitation in the content of his response. 'As an ordinary Christian who has struggled to understand, expound, relate and apply the word of God,' he said. His huge output, and the grasp of Scripture which lay behind it, had been won only through 'daily dogged discipline'.

It became his pattern to rise early to read and pray, and to listen to the BBC World Service news. Listening to God through scripture should not be removed from world events. As we practise 'double-listening', he would say, we can apply the word of God to his world. John Stott's early start to each day gave cause for what became known as his HHH (horizontal half hour) which became his HH (horizontal hour) in later years.

He loved children, and enjoyed being an uncle, a great uncle, and a godfather. While he considered marriage twice, he sensed it was not God's will for him and he resolved not to marry. He also resolved not to pursue an academic career, or to become a bishop. Each decision brought its cost, but his ministry required freedom from the responsibilities these callings would place on him.

John Stott worked hard to be rooted in the eternal gospel and to apply it, for each decade and each context, – with intellectual and theological rigour, perceptiveness, cultural sensitivity, and an eye to the future.

The story of his influence cannot be told without reference to Frances Whitehead. They formed, in the words of Chris Wright, 'one of the greatest partnerships in church history'. It is widely agreed that John could not have achieved half of what he did without Frances at his side. She was a young Christian, working at the BBC, when in 1956 John Stott asked her to become his secretary,[18] and she remained in that position for 55 years. She became 'Auntie Frances' to hundreds who corresponded with 'Uncle John'. We begin this collection with her tribute at the Memorial service in St Paul's Cathedral which, at John's request, was the first to be delivered.

The global influence of this pastor, leader, seminal thinker, friend to thousands, and author of over 50 books, will unfold as future church history is written.

## Editor

18. The job title 'John Stott's Secretary', as it would later appear on Frances's letterhead, was understated. See *John Stott's Right Hand: The untold story of Frances Whitehead* by the current editor, a story John Stott hoped would one day be told. (Expanded and updated edition Dictum /EFAC, 2020.) Chris Wright's quote taken from Thanksgiving service (June, 2109). Available on YouTube.

# TRIBUTE FROM JOHN STOTT'S SECRETARY

## Frances Whitehead

So many tributes from all over the world have been paid to John Stott. I have asked myself what could I say that has not already been said, by way of thanks to God for John's life, and what it has meant to me and so many others? Let me simply express my gratitude for John himself, his godly example, and his faithful preaching through which the light of Christ first dawned on me.

Because I worked alongside him as his secretary for 55 years, perhaps I more than anybody can testify to the fact that, in his case, familiarity, far from breeding contempt, bred the very opposite – a deep respect, and one which inspired belief in God. The more I observed his life and shared it with him, the more I appreciated the genuineness of his faith in Christ, so evident in his consuming passion for the glory of God, and his desire to conform his own life to the will of God. It was an authentic faith that fashioned his life – it gave him a servant heart and a deep compassion for all those in need, one that moved him to keep looking for ways in which he might be of encouragement and support to others, sharing his friendship and his own resources.

To work with John was to watch a hard-working man of great discipline and self-denial, but at the same time to see a life full of grace and warmth. His standards were high and he took trouble over all that he did; nothing was ever slapdash. He was consistent in every way and always kept his word. Although so gifted himself, he never made me feel inferior or unimportant. Instead, he would share and discuss his thoughts and plans with his study assistant and me, listening to our contributions, and eager to ensure consensus between the three of us – the 'happy triumvirate' as he would dub us. So I found him easy to please and ever grateful for one's service.

*HE WOULD SHARE AND DISCUSS HIS THOUGHTS AND PLANS WITH US – THE 'HAPPY TRIUMVIRATE'*

The Scriptures lay at the heart of all John's teaching and preaching. His ability to interpret them was not simply a matter of the intellect, but of a heart full of love for Christ, and a longing to serve him faithfully, no matter what the cost in human terms. For he believed in, and submitted himself to, the sovereignty of God and the Lordship of Christ in his own life – and he accepted the authority of the Bible as the word of God, regardless of ridicule by some.

Indeed, John taught and practised what he believed, and I thank God for the way he pointed me constantly to Jesus. 'Don't look at me', he would say. 'Look at Jesus and listen to him.' But he also demonstrated the truth of what he was saying by his own example of obedience. This was the powerful magnet that drew people to put their faith in Christ as the Son of God and Saviour of the world. He believed that Christ lived on earth, died on the cross for our salvation, and will come again one day in glory. He believed that death is not the end, and that there will be a new creation in which we may all share, through repentance and faith in Jesus.

Thank God that John deeply believed all these truths, lived in the light of them, and maintained them, right to the very end. John's life was a wonderful example of what it means to be a true Christian – and what a blessing he was to all those who were privileged to know him.

*Frances Whitehead was named in John Stott's Will as his 'Friend and Executor'. She also served as a literary executor, and then as a consultant to the literary executors. Frances was awarded a Lambeth MA by Archbishop George Carey in 2001.*

# PART II

# JOHN STOTT:
# ANGLICAN EVANGELICAL

# JOHN STOTT AND THE CHURCH OF ENGLAND

## Timothy Dudley-Smith

John Stott was baptized, confirmed and ordained in the Church of England. It was an Anglican church, All Souls, Langham Place, where he attended as a child and went on to serve as assistant curate, Rector and Rector Emeritus through all his ministry. His funeral service was held in All Souls, and the Thanksgiving Service in St Paul's, the cathedral of the Diocese of London, his 'home diocese' for all his ninety years.

He was never a Prebendary of St Paul's as other All Souls rectors have been, never a member of the Church of England General Synod, never a bishop. But two of our most distinguished contemporary church historians, David Edwards and Adrian Hastings,[19] have given their assessments in unmistakable terms. David Edwards described him as, apart from Archbishop William Temple, 'the most influential clergyman in the Church of England during the twentieth century'.

---

19. David L Edwards, a senior Anglican, served as Chaplain to the Speaker of the House of Commons, and as Bishop of Southwark. In 1988 he engaged John Stott in a liberal-evangelical dialogue to determine the essentials of the Christian faith. It was a model of mutual respect. Adrian Hastings, Professor of Theology at Leeds University, served in Africa and in the UK, as a priest and as an academic.

He places John Stott, therefore, firmly in the Anglican scene, and is right to do so.

One has only to think of the structures that John Stott created to fulfil his vision of a renewed evangelicalism. Consider the Evangelical Fellowship in the Anglican Communion (EFAC), the Church of England Evangelical Council (CEEC), the great National Evangelical Anglican Congresses (NEAC) of 1967 and 1977. Again and again, sometimes privately and sometimes publicly, we find John Stott taking a lead for Scriptural standards in the affairs of the Church of England: heading a delegation to the Archbishops over Reservation of the Sacrament, or offering cogent comments on the Anglican / Roman Catholic Agreed Statements, or sustaining a continuing critique of the Anglican / Methodist proposals for reunion, or the major liturgical revisions of the 1960s and 1970s.

His commitment to the church of his baptism, and his concern for many younger evangelical clergy who looked to him for leadership, is what lay behind the confrontation between Dr Martyn Lloyd-Jones as speaker and John Stott as chairman of the National Assembly of Evangelicals in October 1966. John Stott felt bound to use (some felt, to misuse) his position in the chair to resist a call by the speaker for his hearers, 'especially the ministers and clergy' among them, to leave the major denominations and form a united church.[20]

---

20. For a full account of this incident, see *John Stott: A Global Ministry*, pp65-69.

Among John Stott's heroes was Charles Simeon, the Anglican divine, minister of Holy Trinity Church, Cambridge from 1783 to 1836, whose mark is on Cambridge still. John Stott

## AMONG JOHN STOTT'S HEROES WAS CHARLES SIMEON

edited an anthology of Simeon's sermons, for Simeon, like John Stott, was first and foremost a man of the Scriptures; but they also shared a love for their church. Simeon is well-known for declaring that 'the finest sight short of heaven would be a whole congregation using the prayers of the Liturgy in the true spirit of them.' John Stott was to write in the 1960s about a proposed Prayer Book revision, that the *Book of Common Prayer* (still substantially as Simeon knew it) was 'a precious heritage', and its Holy Communion service 'deeply satisfying to the hearts and minds of generations of churchmen'. Twenty years later he wrote, 'I am deeply grateful to be a member and a minister' of the Church of England, 'and to be able to remain such with good conscience.' He was by no means blind to his church's faults and shortcomings (which he explored in the same article) but while the Church of England remained in its formularies a church loyal to Scripture, he was thankful to continue as a loyal member.

Adrian Hastings, Professor of Theology at the University of Leeds, affirmed that John Stott 'must be accounted one of the most influential figures in the Christian world, standing as he did at the point of intersection of the evangelical movement and the Church of England'. That phrase 'point of intersection' reminds us that John Stott, both in England and on the world stage, was an Anglican evangelical rather than an evangelical Anglican. This distinction is so crucial that

*JOHN WAS AN ANGLICAN EVANGELICAL RATHER THAN AN EVANGELICAL ANGLICAN*

it is best to quote John Stott's own summary of his position. It begins his chapter, 'I believe in the Church of England' in Gavin Reid (ed) *Hope for the Church of England?*[21]

Let me begin by spelling out my priorities. *First* and foremost, by God's sheer mercy, I am a Christian seeking to follow Jesus Christ. *Next*, I am an evangelical Christian because of my conviction that evangelical principles (especially *sola scriptura* and *sola gratia*) are integral to authentic Christianity, and that to be an evangelical Christian is to be a New Testament Christian, and *vice versa*. *Thirdly*, I am an Anglican evangelical Christian, since the Church of England is the particular historical tradition or denomination to which I belong. But I am not an Anglican first, since denominationalism is hard to defend. It seems to me correct to call oneself an Anglican evangelical (in which evangelical is the noun and Anglican the descriptive adjective) rather than an evangelical Anglican (in which Anglican is the noun and evangelical the adjective).

21. Kingsway, 1986 p17.

The evidence for this is not far to seek. It can be seen in his writing (some fifty books and many articles and papers), almost all of which cross denominational and geographical divides, uniting those concerned to understand Scripture and to follow Jesus Christ as Lord. Again, consider John Stott's involvement with a huge range of interdenominational societies and movements: Scripture Union, UCCF, IFES, Evangelical Alliance, Tearfund, Bible Society, his own Evangelical Literature Trust, and the whole of the Lausanne Movement for World Evangelization. Or think of the great university missions. Their aim was to win men and women for Christ, not for any church affiliation. And in his ceaseless missionary journeys overseas, John Stott could be found teaching the Bible under Baptist auspices in Eastern Europe or in the Mar Thoma church in India, as readily as in the Episcopalian context in Australia.

In the Preface to his celebrated book of broadcast talks *Mere Christianity*,[22] C S Lewis wrote of himself:

> The reader should be warned that I offer no help to anyone who is hesitating between two Christian 'denominations'. You will not learn from me whether you ought to become an Anglican, a Methodist, a Presbyterian... This omission is intentional (even in the list I have just given the order is alphabetical). There is no mystery about my own position. I am a very ordinary layman of the Church of England.'

---

22. First published 1952. Now a C S Lewis Signature Classic.

Apart from 'layman', those who read John Stott's legacy in print today will find that, with few exceptions, he could say much the same. Not invariably so, perhaps (remember that 'point of intersection') but very nearly so.

And now, of course, those issues are behind him. I do not know whether John Stott knew the story of George Whitefield in Philadelphia, but I expect he did. David Edwards[23] tells how Whitefield was preaching from a balcony when he looked upwards and cried out 'Father Abraham, whom have you in heaven? Any Episcopalians? Presbyterians? Independents or Seceders? Have you any Methodists? And the answer came, according to Whitefield: 'We don't know those names here.'

*The Rt Revd Timothy Dudley-Smith, retired Bishop of Thetford, hymnwriter, and authorized biographer, was a long-time friend of John Stott from Cambridge days. He preached at the Memorial service in St Paul's Cathedral.*

---

23. Quoting from John Gillies in his *Memoirs of the life of the Revd George Whitefield* (1774).

# JOHN STOTT AND EFAC

## Henry Scriven

For those of us brought up within the evangelical wing of the Church of England, John Stott was famous for his clash with Dr Martyn Lloyd-Jones on 18th October 1966 at the Second National Assembly of Evangelicals. We need to see this in context.

The Anglican Church was John Stott's home for his whole life. From early on in his ministry, he became concerned for the worldwide church and the growth of the Anglican Communion outside England. He delighted in its extension to what are today 40 different Provinces with six 'Extra Provincials',[24] spread across the globe. The Church of England was, he said, an historical church, a confessional church, a national church and a liturgical church.[25]

Many Anglican Provinces grew out of the missionary work of Church of England agencies such as the Church Mission Society, the South American Mission Society, and what is now Crosslinks,[26] which all came from its

---

24. 'Extra Provincials' are dioceses and churches which are part of the Communion, but do not belong to a Province for geographical, political or historical reasons.

25. See *The Living Church* (IVP, 2007) pp 154-165; and *Balanced Christianity* (IVP, 1975 & 2014) pp62, 63.

26. Formerly the Bible Churchman's Missionary Society, BCMS.

evangelical wing. The vision of the new Evangelical Fellowship in the Anglican Communion (EFAC), founded in 1961 was to see evangelical Anglicanism flourish.

## THE VISION OF EFAC WAS TO SEE EVANGELICAL ANGLICANISM FLOURISH

'The driving force and inspiration [for EFAC] came from John Stott', notes his authorized biographer, Timothy Dudley-Smith.[27] 'He had seen in his travels that evangelicals in different parts of the Anglican Communion were facing similar problems, sometimes in positions of considerable isolation; and his growing worldwide correspondence underlined the need for some such structured 'network' as the projected Fellowship would provide.'

John Stott made the distinction between Anglicanism ('largely an historical phenomenon') and evangelicalism ('a theological heritage'). He defined the five main aims of EFAC as (i) fostering fellowship; (ii) bearing witness to biblical principles and principles of the Reformation; (iii) formulating policy; and (iv) exchanging news and information.[28] He used his large number of contacts around the world to build the new Fellowship so that, by the end of the 1960s, EFAC had nearly 20 group members.[29]

---

27. *John Stott: A Global Ministry*, p51.

28. *Ibid*, p52.

29. See Worldwide Evangelical Anglicanism in *Evangelicals Today*, (Lutterworth, 1973), Ed John King.

Its founding member was the Church of England Evangelical Council (CEEC) which was itself formed in 1960, also by John Stott and several others in the Church of England Group of the Inter Varsity Fellowship (now UCCF). Stott invited his old friend Dick Lucas to become Secretary. The reason given for this move in closing down the Anglican group in the Inter Varsity Fellowship and forming a new network, was 'to create a public body, one of whose main aims was to help create an International Fellowship...'[30]

John Stott became the main driver of two new projects that grew out of EFAC in the early years.

*JOHN STOTT BECAME THE MAIN DRIVER OF TWO NEW PROJECTS*

The first was the Christian Foundation series: small books on key issues for the church and its ministry, published by Hodder and Stoughton. Some might see these books, though varying in quality, as the beginning of the phenomenal popularity of Hodder Christian paperbacks which nourished Christians of my generation.

The second was the work of the EFAC Bursary Committee. The object was to give clergy from the younger churches of Africa and Asia the opportunity to come to the UK for theological study and experience of the English church. This became a cooperative effort of colleges and parishes: the colleges reduced their fees, and the parishes sponsored the individuals. Of

30. Minutes of the first meeting of CEEC, quoted in *A Global Ministry*, p56.

course, this gave rise to solid, long-lasting friendships, and many EFAC Bursars became significant leaders in the life of their churches, and in the Communion itself. The EFAC Bursary scheme was the model used later by the Langham Scholars which continues to be most successful.

In the decades following its foundation, John Stott stayed very much involved in EFAC, serving as its Joint Honorary General Secretary, with Jack Dain, Bishop of Sydney. He met with many leaders as he travelled the world or when leaders passed through London. Meetings of the International Council were rare but local fellowships maintained their own life encouraged by their founder. Australia was deeply involved from the beginning, and in the USA the Fellowship of Witness[31] was prominent in the founding of Trinity Episcopal School for Ministry.[32] This was fully accredited by The Episcopal Church (TEC) and, after the formation of the Anglican Church in North America (ACNA) in 2009, it became used by both the Episcopal Church and ACNA for the training of ministers.

In the summer of 1993, EFAC mounted a major international consultation in Canterbury on the theme of the Anglican Communion and Scripture.[33] *The Church Times* gave most of a page to a summary of its Report,

31. The forerunner of EFAC USA.

32. Ambridge, just outside Pittsburgh, Pennsylvania.

33. Under the leadership of Bishop David Evans, formerly Bishop of Peru and General Secretary, South American Mission Society.

calling it 'a ringing statement of mainstream Anglican evangelical attitudes to the Bible'.[34] Dudley Smith sums up: 'Such a Consultation would have been unthinkable in the days before EFAC: or indeed in its early days as a struggling and at times fragile consortium. For more than twenty years it remained the kind of institution aptly described as 'the lengthened shadow of one man'. Canterbury 1993 suggests that in the global village of our shrinking world, the Fellowship will have a continuing, and perhaps increasing, part to play.'

From 1993 onwards there were further such theological consultations, though on a smaller scale, addressing issues from Anthropology to the Family, from International Relations to Mission.[35] These meetings of EFAC's Theological Resource Network (TRN) drew leaders from many different contexts to look at issues of critical concern for Anglican evangelicals. These gatherings were followed by some quiet years, before the 2019 consultation in Uganda, on the delicate issue of 'Corruption in Church and Society'. Further consultations will enable continued sharing of biblical insights on urgent contemporary topics.

EFAC played a key role in the 1998 Lambeth Conference, as the Anglican Church entered

*EFAC PLAYED A KEY ROLE IN THE 1998 LAMBETH CONFERENCE*

---

34. *A Global Ministry*, p299.

35. Hosted in South Africa (1995), Jamaica (1997), Nigeria (1999) Malaysia (2001), and Kenya (2003).

what became a crisis in the Communion over human sexuality. The famous 1998 Resolution 1:10 owed much to the work of EFAC in co-ordinating the majority of attending bishops who were clearly and boldly upholding evangelical faith and practice.

EFAC today, like its founding English affiliate CEEC, is very aware of being a vital part of the ongoing work of the Anglican Church in the world. Evangelicals have been marginalised in parts of the world that are focusing more on how to relate to modern culture than on the demands of Scripture. The fruit of its biblical witness is plain to see in thriving congregations and growing dioceses, real needs being met by the living God, and lives transformed by a living hope in the resurrection of Jesus.

It is not an easy road to travel. There are many forces working against us. EFAC has never been a large, influential body and CEEC is just a part of the larger and more diverse Church of England. But the strength of each is in the faithfulness of its members and its deep roots in the Bible, and the history and traditions of the church. We have a goodly heritage (Psalm 16:6). Our prayer is that we might continue to be gracious but firm and clear, in the spirit of our founder, John Stott.

*The Rt Revd Henry Scriven is the General Secretary of EFAC. He was successively Suffragan Bishop in Europe, Assistant Bishop of Pittsburgh, and Latin America Director with the Church Mission Society.*

# AN ENCOURAGEMENT TO THE LOCAL CHURCH IN WALES

**Bill Lewis**

John Stott travelled the world as a teacher, preacher and evangelist, but a little corner of Pembrokeshire, South West Wales, held a special place in his affection. The Hookses, a one-time farmhouse in Dale, whose land had been requisitioned for a wartime airfield, was home from home for about three months each year. While in seclusion there he wrote most of his books, but he also found time to support the local church.

He regularly attended worship in the local parish church, along with guests at The Hookses. This was much appreciated by the local people.

In the 1950s and 1960s evangelicals were few and far between in the Church in Wales, virtually an endangered species, and generally regarded as being non-conformists at heart and not true Anglicans. John was concerned about this,

*EVANGELICALS WERE VIRTUALLY AN ENDANGERED SPECIES*

and he resolved to 'do something about it'. He lobbied the Archbishop of Wales, but he also decided to invite the few evangelicals known to him to an annual day of teaching and fellowship at The Hookses; some drove a hundred miles to find an oasis of spiritual blessing in barren times. Out of those meetings was founded the Evangelical Fellowship in the Church in Wales (EFCW) in March 1967, of which I was the first secretary, with 28 members. For thirty years or more the 'Dale Days' were a constant source of encouragement and affirmation, and helped members of EFCW to play an increasingly significant part in the life of the Church in Wales. Now in 2020 some EFCW members have become Bishops, some Archdeacons, and several parishes are doing excellent work in evangelism and discipleship. Indeed it is fair to say that most of the churches which are growing are evangelical, at a time when many churches are slowly fading to nothing.

In 1970 John offered to give a lecture on 'An unchanging gospel in a changing world' for the ministers and clergy of Pembrokeshire. The Bishop was invited to chair the meeting: he was new in post, very much an Anglo-Catholic, and rather suspicious of anything evangelical. He accepted with some hesitation, met John over lunch, listened to a gracious, brilliant and highly-relevant lecture, and his whole attitude changed. Prejudice is overcome, not by argument or criticising one another from the safety of entrenched positions, but by gracious engagement on a personal level.

*PREJUDICE IS OVERCOME, ENTRENCHED BY GRACIOUS ENGAGEMENT*

I, along with many others, have good reason to be grateful to John for his books, his teaching and his constant encouragement of local church ministry. One special memory I have is of the time he came to preach for me in St Giles, Letterston in 1971. His sermon was a clear and winsome exposition of the gospel, but the thing which impressed me most was to watch him in the after-church 'bun fight', no top table for this Queen's chaplain and international ambassador for Christ:  far from it, he was wandering around, cup of tea in hand, speaking to as many of the village people as possible, following the example of Jesus, as 'one who came, not to be served, but to serve'.

Soon after I arrived in the village, on my first pastoral visit to the home of the local Squire, I was asked whom I thought 'worth knowing'. (My answer to this question would have been 'about a thousand people' *ie* the whole population.) Then the Squire's wife suggested the name of the Justice of the Peace, who happened to be a very faithful church member, whom I already knew. As I already knew her, I became kosher! How different was our guest preacher; to him everyone in the room was worth knowing!

In 2005, six years before his death, John decided to invite ministers and clergy from Pembrokeshire to a day of teaching at The Hookses, twice a year; this was attended by up to thirty grateful people. A few times he spoke himself, though frail, and this spoke volumes about faithfulness to the end. The mantle for this, as with several other ministries, has fallen on Chris Wright.

Christians in Pembrokeshire find it very moving that John decided that his final earthly resting place should be the village cemetery in Dale, about half a mile from The Hookses. I led the service for the interment of ashes, in the village church of St James the Great where he and Frances Whitehead and visitors to The Hookses so often worshipped.

John asked for the following words, echoing the tribute to Charles Simeon in Holy Trinity Church, Cambridge, to be inscribed on a gravestone of Welsh slate.

*Buried here are the ashes of*
*JOHN R W STOTT*
*(1921-2011)*
*Rector of All Souls Church*
*Langham Place, London 1950-1975*
*Rector Emeritus 1975-2011*

*Who resolved*
*Both as the ground of his salvation*
*And as the subject of his ministry*
*To know nothing except*
*JESUS CHRIST*
*And him crucified*
*(1 Corinthians 2:2)*

*Revd Bill Lewis spent 35 years in parish ministry, and served for five years as Provincial Officer for Evangelism and Adult Education in the Church in Wales.*

# PART III

# GLOBAL INTER-DENOMINATIONAL MINISTRY

# 'ABRAHAMIC AND APOSTOLIC' MINISTRY

**Chris Wright**

Chris Wright sets the scene for the founding of
Langham Partnership International

'I am a great believer,' John Stott would say, 'in the
importance of BBC. Not the British Broadcasting
Corporation, nor Bethlehem Bible College, nor even
Beautiful British Columbia. But Balanced Biblical
Christianity.'

I would like to suggest that the scale and scope of
John Stott's ministry within the global church rested on
his biblical balance of Old and New Testaments. He was
both Abrahamic and apostolic. Let me explain.

## JOHN STOTT'S MISSION WAS 'APOSTOLIC' IN NATURE

John would never have claimed
the title 'apostle' for himself.
'There are no apostles in today's
church,' he said, 'with the same
status or authority as the unique
apostles of the Lord Jesus Christ
in the New Testament.' But his ministry was apostolic
in the sense that it faithfully reflected the passion

*HIS MINISTRY FAITHFULLY REFLECTED THE PASSION AND PRIORITIES OF THE APOSTLES* and priorities of the biblical apostles: evangelism and teaching.

## (i) EVANGELISM

The apostles proclaimed the good news that Jesus of Nazareth was the promised Messiah and Lord, and called people to receive the salvation God had accomplished through his cross and resurrection by repentance, faith and obedience.

John Stott had the heart of an evangelist from his own teenage conversion to his final years in the College of St Barnabas. While still at Rugby School he was helping to run evangelistic camps for boys at Iwerne Minster,[36] and giving talks to lead others to the Saviour. About a year before he died, he told me with some excitement of how he had been able to 'explain the way of salvation' to one of his carers – a woman who asked him a question while wheeling him back from lunch in the dining room. The first of John's international travels (1956-57) was to conduct evangelistic missions on university campuses in the USA and Canada, and for years his effectiveness as a university evangelist was the main reason for his growing international

36. His leadership gifts were recognized straight away by E J H Nash (commonly known as 'Bash'), founder of the camps for boys from the top public schools; these were known in shorthand as 'Iwerne' from their base in Iwerne Minster, Dorset. It was here that John Stott cut his teeth as a spiritual leader. Bash discipled John as a young Christian, and was to him, in John's words, 'a philospher and a friend'. (See *A study in spiritual power*, Ed John Eddison, 1983.) John Stott always maintained that the greatest spiritual influences on his life had been 'Iwerne and the CICCU'.

ministry. His early book *Basic Christianity* distilled those evangelistic addresses, and has led thousands of people to faith in Christ. And his last book, *The Radical Disciple*, written when he could scarcely hold his pen steady, still breathes the truth and the appeal of the apostolic gospel.

## (ii) TEACHING

The apostles were tireless in teaching their new churches, by visiting them and writing to them, to ground them in their faith and urge them to grow up in maturity in Christ. In this, just as much as in evangelism, they were doing what Jesus told them in 'the great commission', that is, 'teaching them to obey all that I have commanded you'.

John Stott was as passionate and committed to the work of apostolic teaching as to apostolic evangelism.

Like the Apostle Paul, he longed to see Christians and churches growing up to maturity in Christ, and growing into the likeness of Christ. He saw and rejoiced in the numerical growth of the church in the Majority World.[37] But he lamented the lack of teaching, discipling and pastoral leadership that left new churches weak and vulnerable, plagued by spiritual extremism and moral laxity, and at the mercy of self-appointed leaders, exploiting the flock with more greed than

37. This was long before such a term was used, or the phenomenal growth of the church in the Global South had been brought to the attention of Christians in the West, through books like *The Next Christendom* by Philip Jenkins (Third edition, Oxford University Press, 2011).

grace. Like the Apostle John, he longed for Christians and churches to live in love and unity, and saw our chronic dividedness (particularly among some evangelicals) as visible evidence of immaturity.

*HE LONGED FOR CHRISTIANS AND CHURCHES TO LIVE IN LOVE AND UNITY*

## THE 'LANGHAM LOGIC'

'How would you sum up the state of the Church around the world today?' he would often ask, when introducing the work of the Langham Partnership. 'I can do it in three words, *Growth without depth*. There is much evangelistic growth in numbers. But sadly there is also shallowness and immaturity everywhere, and it is not pleasing to God.' From that challenging start he would go on to articulate what he called the 'Langham Logic', based on three biblical convictions (supported with many biblical texts) and a logical conclusion.

i)   God wants his church to grow up, not just to grow bigger
ii)  God's church grows through God's word
iii) God's word comes to God's people mainly (not exclusively) through biblical preaching

In essence: if God wants his people to grow to maturity (which he does); if the Church grows through God's word (which it does); if God's word comes to God's people through faithful preaching (which it does); then the logical question to ask is, 'What can we do to raise the standards of biblical preaching?' For then the word of God will feed the people of God, and they will grow to maturity, and thereby grow in effectiveness in their mission and their ministry.

This rationale remains the driving engine of Langham Partnership International, which John founded. It began as the Langham Trust in 1969. (Characteristically named, not after himself, but the street where All Souls stands.) This trust provided scholarships to help gifted younger evangelicals gain doctorates and thus be better equipped to teach pastors in their own countries. Next came the Evangelical Literature Trust in 1971, recycling John's own book royalties and other donations to provide books for pastors and for seminary libraries, to strengthen biblical preaching. And finally in 2001 John and I pioneered some preaching seminars in Latin America, to motivate and train pastors in the skills of biblical expository preaching. These three initiatives now work together as three programmes: Langham Scholars, Langham Literature and Langham Preaching, under the unifying vision, *'To see churches worldwide equipped for mission and growing to maturity in Christ through the ministry of pastors and leaders who believe, teach, and live by, the word of God.'*

- *Langham Scholars* enables men and women from the Majority World to gain doctorates. Most then teach future generations of pastors in Bible Colleges and seminaries. Partly as the fruit of this work, new high-quality evangelical seminaries now offer doctoral degrees in Majority World countries. Langham alumni, serving on faculties, nurture future Langham scholars.

- *Langham Literature* provides evangelical books to hundreds of thousands of pastors, and hundreds of seminary libraries. This began with mainly western books in English or translation. Now Langham is increasingly helping to foster indigenous evangelical writers, and editors, with the establishing of new publishing houses in Majority World countries. These writers and editors feed the minds and hearts of their own people in their own languages, and resource pastors and preachers for their primary task. An early flagship was the one-volume *Africa Bible Commentary* written entirely by African scholars for African contexts. Its first edition in English was soon followed by editions in French, Portuguese, Swahili and Malagasy, with plans put in place for Amharic and Hausa. Since then Langham Literature has sponsored comparable volumes in South Asia, Latin America, and the Arabic-speaking world.

- *Langham Preaching* is creating movements for biblical preaching in more than sixty countries. Here we work with church leaders to arrange

(i) training seminars, (ii) local preachers' clubs, (iii) the training of local and national facilitators and trainers, (iv) regional conferences, and (v) the provision of books and other preaching resources. Alongside this we are working to raise the standard of how preaching is taught in seminaries.

All of these ministries are an expression of 'apostolic teaching', whether that teaching happens in a pulpit, in a classroom, or through the pages of a book. They are comparable to the ministries of Apollos (a scholar teacher), Timothy (a preacher and trainer of others) and even Tertius (a trained scribe who wrote Paul's letter to the Romans). All teaching which builds the church (theological education in its broadest sense), is part of the great commission, so is by its nature, missional. There is mission beyond evangelism: the mission of teaching and discipling.

## JOHN STOTT'S CALL WAS 'ABRAHAMIC'

As we gain perspective on John's ministry, we see two ways in which he mirrored Abraham. The first is the most obvious.

### a) BLESSING THE NATIONS

According to Paul, the gospel was announced in advance to Abraham.[38] This good news of God's promise to bless all nations on earth was ultimately fulfilled

38. Galatians 3:8.

through Jesus Christ, and the spread of his gospel to all nations. But the role of God's people has always been 'Abrahamic' in the sense of being *instrumental* in God fulfilling that promise.

In that sense, John Stott was truly Abahamic. His whole life, from a very early stage of his pastoral ministry, was spent in reaching out to the nations of the world. His travels in all continents were not just some kind of tourism for Jesus (or sanctified bird-watching). His passion was to gain a global understanding of Christian theology and mission, of what it meant to be the worldwide body of Christ. Wherever he went, he did as his father had told him as a small boy in the countryside – he kept his eyes and ears open. He

*HE WAS A BLESSING TO SO MANY BECAUSE HE OPENED HIMSELF UP TO BE BLESSED BY THEM*

listened respectfully to other cultures, learned from them, and sought to see the richness of the eternal biblical gospel through the eyes, needs and aspirations of others. It could be said that he was a blessing to so many, in every part of the world, because he opened himself up to be blessed by them.

The extent to which John Stott was Abrahamic in being a 'blessing to the nations' can be seen in the number of international evangelical bodies with which he had close association – the Lausanne Movement,

World Evangelical Alliance, IFES, Scripture Union,[39] A Rocha, Tearfund...

*b) THE OBEDIENCE OF FAITH*

John's ministry was Abrahamic not just in its *scope*, but also in its *substance*. 'By faith Abraham...obeyed.'[40] God's promise came with a demand, that he should walk in the way of the Lord by doing righteousness and justice, and teaching his household to do the same.[41] God's people were to be a means of blessing the nations by living among them in a way that was ethically distinctive at all levels – political, economic, judicial, familial, sexual, *etc*. God's people are to be, as Jesus put it, salt in a corrupt world and light in a dark world. We can perform that function only by being engaged with every area over which Jesus is Lord. (This means *every* area of life on earth, and even the earth itself as God's creation.)

John Stott was as passionate about the engagement and penetration of the gospel in the everyday public arena, as he was about its truth. He could not separate them. He would have argued that the truth of the gospel had not been grasped until its radical demands, as well as its gracious promises, were

---

39. He served as President of Scripture Union England and Wales 1965-1973. While not listing offices for each ministry, we do so for SU, given the importance of E J H Nash in his life.

40. Genesis 12:1-4; Hebrews 11:8.

41. Genesis 18:19.

being presented and lived out by 'integrated Christians'. His rejection of the disabling falsehood of a 'sacred-secular divide' led to his founding the London Institute for Contemporary Christianity.

*JOHN WAS NOT INTERESTED IN 'THE IRREDUCIBLE MINIMUM OF THE GOSPEL*

John was not interested in 'the irreducible minimum of the gospel'. He wanted to be faithful to the whole biblical gospel in all its glorious richness and in its transforming power, which brings all of life in heaven and earth under the Lordship of Christ.

In this conviction, and in all he did to give it practical expression, John Stott was Abrahamic and apostolic. The global church has been incalculably blessed through him in both respects. We have much yet to learn and to implement.

*Christopher J H Wright, widely known as an Old Testament theologian, author and speaker, is International Director of Langham Partnership International, and former Chair of the Lausanne Theology Working Group.*

# SERVING THE
# STUDENT WORLD

**Lindsay Brown**

John Stott spent the war years from 1940 in Cambridge, first at Trinity College, where he gained a double first in modern languages and theology, and then at the Anglican training college, Ridley Hall. Over these years, foundations were being laid for his life's ministry.

His father, a major general in the medical corps, felt a sense of embarrassment that John should spend these days in academia, instead of helping the war effort. But John was firm: as a Christian, he believed he had to be a pacifist. In years to come, he saw that his position was not well informed. No-one had helped him understand the Just War theory. Had he engaged with it, he sensed he would have responded differently. It proved costly for him as it caused grief for his family. Throughout his ministry, he always wanted Christian students to be better helped to formulate ethical judgments than he had been.

*AS WE LOOK BACK, WE SEE GOD'S WONDERFUL PROVIDENCE EVEN IN OUR MISTAKES*

As we look back, we see God's wonderful hand of providence even in our mistakes. In John's first week, he made friends with a zoologist, Oliver Barclay, two years his senior. They spent much time together in discussion, walking round and round Trinity Great Court, or along the Backs of the colleges, 'trying to solve all the problems of Church and state'. Friendships built in student years can last for life; the friendship between John Stott and Oliver Barclay was one such friendship.

Both were immersed in the life of the CICCU and both would serve as its lifelong Honorary Vice-Presidents. After Oliver Barclay completed his doctorate, he moved to London to take a new position as Assistant General Secretary in the Inter-Varsity Fellowship (now UCCF). Its founding General Secretary was Douglas Johnson. John Stott had great respect for 'DJ', as he was always known, and would refer to him fifty years later as the greatest single influence on UK evangelicalism in the 20th Century.[42]

### INTER-VARSITY PRESS

Through Oliver Barclay and Douglas Johnson, John Stott met Ronald Inchley, who, as a recent graduate, had founded in 1936 what became Inter-Varsity Press (IVP). Ronald Inchley, known as 'RI', nurtured John as a young author. At that time evangelicals were rather derided. This new publishing house, getting started again after the war, was a modest venture. Inchley, who read English at Birmingham, spent much of the war as a

---

42. 'What are the challenges to evangelicalism at the end of the 20th Century?' Word Alive, 1993.

quantity surveyor employed by John Laing Construction, building airfields. Here he learned the delicate balance of costing time and materials against outcome, a new idea in an organization more concerned with ministry than management. He set the publishing venture on a sound footing, and had a shrewd eye for new authors. Soon his list was to include the sharpest evangelical thinkers of the day.[43]

From small beginnings, this operation to produce books for students and graduates was to gain wide credibility in the evangelical church globally. Inter-Varsity Press would become John Stott's main publisher. In addition to the 34 titles it published by him, IVP also published the widely-popular *Bible Speaks Today* (BST) series, of which John Stott was founder and New Testament editor. His books would go into sixty languages.

## UNIVERSITY MISSIONS
The All Souls Church Council gave generously of their pastor's time. For a quarter of a century, starting and ending in his Alma Mater (1952, 1977), John Stott led many university missions across the UK, and around the world. He was highly-gifted as a university evangelist.

---

43. For example J I Packer, D J Wiseman, and G T Manley (who was Senior Wrangler (top mathematician) at Cambridge in the year that Bertrand Russell was ranked as sixth); and later Francis Schaeffer. 'He took pleasure in nurturing the skills of new writers, would take them on walks to find out what they wanted to tackle, and then hound them to deliver the goods.' (Obituary in *The Times*, 25 May 2005.)

He loved to remind students that a clearly-reasoned presentation of the gospel acts as a basis or ground for faith. It is not a replacement for the Holy Spirit's working, but a vehicle of the Holy Spirit, a means by which God's objective truth can be made clear.

John brought a rare combination of gifts to campus ministry. He was an evangelist, a teacher, and an able and patient apologist. He would typically proclaim Christian truth in the evenings, by expounding passages from the gospels; then in smaller contexts, often in a faculty or department, he would listen to students' questions, work back with students to the premise of the question, and engage in reasoned dialogue, modelling a robust Christian mind.

*PROFESSIONS OF FAITH WOULD COME GRADUALLY*

Professions of faith would come gradually, some during the mission week, others later, even much later. In his early years as a missioner, he would preach in clerical robes, often in a church building. By 1977 the world was much more secular, and there was no religious structure to the meeting. In the West the venues were, by then, almost all neutral territory. Stott led missions in the following universities, listed here alphabetically. He returned to several of these universities to conduct more than one mission.

*UK*: Aberdeen; Aberystwyth; Cambridge; Durham; Exeter; Leeds; Leicester; Liverpool; London; Loughborough;

Manchester; Newcastle; Nottingham; Oxford; Queen's, Belfast; St Andrews; Trinity College, Dublin.

*Around the world*: Cape Town; Ceylon; Ghana; Harvard; Helsinki; Ibadan; Illinois; Lund; Malaya; Manila; Manitoba; McGill; Melbourne; Michigan; Nairobi; Oslo; Sierra Leone; Singapore; Sydney; Rhodesia [now Zimbabwe] and Nyasaland [now Malawi]; Toronto; Western Ontario; Witwatersrand; Uganda.

In each place, John would be the servant of the student mission committee. The student leaders knew the context and were Christ's aroma in it. He much appreciated the IFES policy of student leadership,[44] and was glad to hold himself accountable to the students. This was, for them, always a wonderfully-memorable learning experience,

> **JOHN WAS GLAD TO HOLD HIMSELF ACCOUNTABLE TO STUDENTS**

not only during the mission week, but in all its preparation, and in working to ground new believers in the faith.

In addition, he was a regular Bible expositor at the Intervarsity (US and Canada) Urbana Missions Conventions. John, a much-loved Urbana speaker, was invited to return once more in 2003, to give the opening address. He was eighty-two years of age. He managed

---

44. That is, that the students themselves lead university groups, with staff giving encouragement and advice.

to join us that summer for the IFES World Assembly in the Netherlands, weaving into the programme his usual schedule of private meetings for those who wanted to talk. Sadly in December ill-health impeded him from going to Urbana, and he had to submit his address, meticulously prepared, to be read for him.[45]

I first met John when I was President of the Christian Union at Oxford. We saw each other often over the years, as I joined UCCF staff, and then served as IFES Regional Secretary for Europe. When John heard news of my appointment in 1991 as IFES General Secretary while still in my thirties, he must have remembered his own feelings in becoming a very young Rector of All Souls. Evangelical student movements had, by that stage, been established in 67 countries, some still very fragile; and much pioneering was still to be done.

The goal of IFES is to make Christ known in every university in the world. This was, John Stott said, 'the most strategic work imaginable'. He remained committed to students all his life. He used prayer diaries from IFES and its British affiliate, UCCF, praying through the student year, with which he was so familiar. John served as Honorary President and Honorary Vice-President of UCCF and IFES several times. The library

---

45. It was read by Joshua Wathanga, then IFES Associate General Secretary. The Convention was named after the city in which it was located for most of its history (on the University of Illinois campus). Urbana 2003 was the final Convention held in Urbana as numbers crept above its 19,000 capacity. It moved to St Louis. These triennial gatherings, held at the end of December, have stirred a mission commitment in the lives of a quarter of a million students since they began after the Second World War.

in Blue Boar House, Oxford, the shared office of both these movements, is named 'Uncle John's Library' after him. His wide travels meant that he got to know staff and students in many nations, and he enjoyed sharing fellowship with them. He rarely travelled anywhere without participating in student ministry.

He wrote me a kind letter on my appointment as General Secretary, as always bringing together pastoral advice and spiritual encouragement. In it he quoted the words of John Newton:

'Lindsay, I hope you will be "a reed in non-essentials and an iron in essentials".'

When we spoke soon afterwards, he called to mind Martin Luther's words when writing on the Apostle Paul, and he urged me to be 'strong in truth and soft in love'. He was referring to the need to stand firm on key doctrines, and to allow breadth in matters which were not central. Our doctrinal basis includes only the primary truths of the gospel, the things 'of first importance'. Matters like church practice are all secondary. We teach students to unite around these primaries, hence the name 'Christian Union', by which campus groups are often known. This primary / secondary distinction was instinctive to John Stott.[46] He

---

46. In 1998, conscious of his advancing years, John Stott began work on *Evangelical Truth: A personal plea for unity*. This appeal to the evangelical church was, in his mind, possibly his last book. It was published by IVP (UK and US) in 1999, his handwriting a distinctive feature in the design, to emphasise its urgent and personal nature. He joined us in July 1999 (in Seoul, Korea) for the quadrennial IFES World Assembly. It was his practice to participate in these gatherings whenever he could manage to do so. We launched the book in Seoul.

was a peacemaker, eirenic, gracious; a listener. But he had an iron backbone. The essentials *were* essential.

*HE WAS EIRENIC, GRACIOUS; A LISTENER. BUT HE HAD AN IRON BACKBONE*

His book *The Cross of Christ*, which he considered his best, left no room for doubt.

John described himself as 'an IFES man' in a video greeting to the IFES World Assembly in 2007. As he was recovering from a fall, he was unable to be there. His message characteristically wasted no syllable. He said: 'I would like to introduce myself to you as a committed "IFES man" – and that for at least four reasons. IFES is (i) Biblical, seeking in all things to be submissive to the supreme authority of scripture; (ii) Indigenous, encouraging self-governing national movements; (iii) Evangelistic, with students winning students for Christ, and (iv) Holistic, seeking to lead new converts to maturity in Christ. So I thank God for IFES.'

Evangelical churches in university towns will always be strategic places for the gospel. The numbers of such ministries were few in the early days, but over the years, not least through the work of John Stott and the leaders of IVF / UCCF, the map changed. New generations of evangelicals, nurtured in the Christian Unions, were gradually filling pulpits.

John was a student at Ridley Hall when Tyndale House was established as a Centre for Biblical Research in 1944. His far-sightedness, even at that age, saw the future implications of this research centre, initiated by Douglas Johnson and his friends. In due course there would be evangelicals teaching in theology faculties of secular universities. Their influence would spill over into Christian publishing, into the local church, into the CUs, and so into the lives of students. These students would soon become Christian graduates in the public arenas. Forming the influencers of the next generation is a serious obligation for the church.

*FORMING INFLUENCERS IS A SERIOUS OBLIGATION FOR THE CHURCH*

In the 1960s and 1970s thousands of international students poured into Britain, especially from the former British colonies, which were now gaining independence. New governments wanted their future leaders to gain a western education. John Stott saw the vital role the UK evangelical church could play in building up Christian students, and in bringing the gospel to many who were not Christians. He established a role on his church staff to develop a specific ministry among international students.

John loved the secular university. While he saw some benefit for US Christian students in enrolling in Christian colleges, it saddened him deeply that so many were being segregated from mainstream university life. He enjoyed engaging with the humanists and the existentialists in university missions, and he loved the creativity and courage shown by students in inviting people to meetings.[47] He urged that Christian students avoid the temptation to withdraw from university life.

*HE URGED THAT CHRISTIAN STUDENTS AVOID 'RABBIT HOLE CHRISTIANITY'*

He referred to what he called 'rabbit hole Christianity'. Here Christians cut themselves off from the world, believing the only worthwhile activity is to evangelize or attend Christian meetings. Rabbits put their heads out of their burrows then, if there is no one about, race across open land and swiftly return to their burrows. Christians can be like that, dashing between Christian activities, with minimal contact with the world. This breeds a hit-and-run form of evangelism that does not respect the integrity of a university, which, for all its student life excesses, is a community of learning.

John Stott urged students to develop what we might call 'a Christian mind', or a Christian worldview.

47. Two brief vignettes from 1959 illustrate this. That year, John Stott was missioner at two of Africa's top universities: University of Cape Town (UCT) and Witwatersrand, Jo'burg ('Wits'). Students at UCT showed unusual creativity in arranging a low-flying plane to drop leaflets to advertise the mission meetings over their steeply-terraced campus. The following week at Wits, the atheists were so incensed at the mission that they disrupted a meeting with placards and loud shouts. John invited the atheist leader to come to the front and, to everyone's surprise, handed him the microphone. There was silence in the Great Hall, all eyes on the platform. Roy Comrie recalls how the student addressed John 'as if he were an ignoramus' and challenged him to a public debate. The invitation was graciously accepted and the date set for the end of the week. The debate was crammed full, everyone attentive, as John Stott responded to each of the proposer's 17 points. The Atheist Society disbanded soon afterwards, and did not reappear in that student generation.

That term was first coined by Professor Daniel Lamont in one of the early conferences of what was to become the global IFES movement, in the 1930s. It was later popularised by the writings of Harry Blamires and John Stott.[48] To develop a Christian mind fulfils three criteria. *First*, it glorifies our Creator who has made us as rational creatures in his own image and wants us to explore his revelation in nature and in scripture. *Secondly*, it enriches our Christian life as we can worship God only when we know who he is, and reflect on his glory. Faith rests on a knowledge of God's character. *Thirdly*, it strengthens our evangelistic witness. Many times in the Book of Acts we read of the apostles reasoning with

*FAITH RESTS ON A KNOWLEDGE OF GOD'S CHARACTER*

people and seeking to persuade them. Faith and reason are not contrasted in scripture; it is faith and sight which are held in contrast. Jesus challenged Thomas to believe 'having not seen', not 'having not thought'.

At John's funeral, His Honour Judge David Turner reflected on his student days at King's College, London, and what it was like to come to All Souls as an eighteen-year-old in the 1970s. He said:

> 'I shall never forget the impact of seeing John kneel to pray in the pulpit before he preached, in

---

48. Harry Blamires, *The Christian Mind* (SPCK, 1963; Servant Books, 1978 USA); John Stott, *Your Mind Matters* (IVP, 1972).

the scarlet cassock of a Queen's Chaplain under a gleaming white surplice. This was expository preaching of exceptional clarity and authority such as I had never heard.

'John treated us as intelligent people. He trained us in "thoughtful allegiance" to scripture. He moved us by his passion. He taught us "double listening" – the need to "hear" the word and the world and to find the connections. He abhorred in equal measure "undevotional theology" (mind without heart) and "untheological devotion" (heart without mind). He was, as he liked to say, "an impenitent believer in the importance of biblical preaching". We loved it!

'Landmark sermon series preached here at All Souls on Romans, Ephesians, Acts, II Timothy, and on Issues Facing Christians, later travelled the world and formed the core of some of John's fifty-one books. As we read those books now, we can still hear the structure of his delivery and the cadences of his voice. We would sometimes joke that John was clearer on the Apostle Paul than was the Apostle Paul!'[49]

I close with a personal conversation in which John was reflecting back on his life, by now in his eighties. He said to me, 'If I could live my life again, I would

---

49. Funeral service available on YouTube.

join you in student ministry.' He stood with Charles Malik (and Martin Luther) as a man who took the university seriously.[50] Like Martyn Lloyd-Jones,[51] John Stott remained close to the IFES student movements, and a constant pastor to its

**IF I COULD LIVE MY LIFE AGAIN, I WOULD JOIN YOU IN STUDENT MINISTRY**

generations of leaders. We thank God for him.

*Lindsay Brown is IFES Evangelist-at-Large, working to raise up a new generation of evangelists in Europe's universities. He served as IFES General Secretary (1991-2007) and as International Director of the Lausanne Movement (2008-2017).*

---

50. 'The Church can render no greater service to itself, or to the cause of the gospel, than to try to recapture the universities for Christ. More potently than by any other means, change the university and you change the world.' Charles Habib Malik in his 1981 Pascal lectures, *A Christian Critique of the University.* Malik had a distinguished career in academia and in the United Nations.

51. Martyn Lloyd-Jones held office from 1947 (when IFES was constituted in Harvard) to the time of his death in 1981; first as Chairman, then as President and Vice-President.

# JOHN STOTT AND THE LAUSANNE MOVEMENT

**Julia Cameron**

As decades pass, history will further unfold the extent of John Stott's influence on theological thinking, on preaching, on the tensions between the gospel and culture, on the development of a Christian mind, on evangelical commitment to social justice, and supremely on world evangelization.

*HIS RELATIONSHIP WITH LAUSANNE COULD BE DESCRIBED AS RECIPROCAL, EVEN SYMBIOTIC*

His relationship with Lausanne,[52] particularly in the period 1974-1996 could well be described as reciprocal, even symbiotic. His multi-faceted ministry fitted the multi-faceted Lausanne aspirations, which he had played no small part in fashioning. Lausanne channels and networks would become a major means through which he influenced the church globally.

In 2006, Doug Birdsall invited John Stott to accept a lifetime title of Honorary Chairman, which he did, with

---

52. Often used as shorthand in speech and writing for the Lausanne Movement, formerly known and still registered as the Lausanne Committee for World Evangelization.

a sense of pleasure. It had been a consistent pattern to accept honorary titles only if he could maintain a lively link with the endeavour, and he followed news of planning for the Third Lausanne Congress with eager interest. Lindsay Brown, who was appointed as Lausanne Movement International Director in 2008, and Chris Wright, who followed in John's own stead as chair of the Lausanne Theology Working Group, were both old friends.

John's personal friendship with Billy Graham from the time of the Cambridge University mission in 1955 led to his being into the early stages of planning for the 1974 International Congress on World Evangelization. This was held in Lausanne, Switzerland, and from this city the Lausanne Movement would take its name. Stott was by this stage already regarded as a leader and figurehead, through participation in World Council of Churches events, and in the 1966 conference on world evangelization in Berlin. The 1970s included seven or

> *LAUSANNE WAS TO HAVE A LION'S SHARE OF HIS TIME*

eight other international conferences. But from 1974, Lausanne was to have a lion's share of his time.

## EDINBURGH 1910 – LEARNING FROM HISTORY

The world missions conference in Edinburgh, in June 1910, convened by John R Mott, a visionary from the US Mid-West with a deep passion for evangelism,

was a remarkable gathering by any criteria. But from
the outset it was flawed through well-intentioned
but ill-considered decisions. In a move to gain the
participation of the then Archbishop of Canterbury,
Randall Thomas Davidson, John Mott agreed that
matters of doctrine would not be discussed. It was a
costly error of judgment. He opened his final address:
'The end of the congress is the beginning of the
conquest', and participants left on this stirring note,
resolved to give their best energy to the glory of Christ
in world evangelization. The two world wars would have
a huge bearing on mission strategy. But the unforeseen
hidden cost for including the Archbishop was regarded
by John Stott as having had even more profound, and

*AS A RESULT,
MISSION
BECAME
SIDELINED IN
THE CHURCH*

longer-lasting, significance.

As central questions on
the content of the gospel, the
theology of evangelism and
the nature of the church were
not on the agenda, Edinburgh
1910 proved a lost opportunity to engage with the
critical theological challenges of the day. Theological
liberalism was to dominate in university faculties and
in seminaries for the next several decades. As a result,
mission became sidelined in the church.[53]

---

53. In 1919 we see, by contrast, the resolve of undergraduates in Cambridge
to maintain the centrality of the Atonement in their definition of the gospel.
This led Norman Grubb and fellow CICCU leaders to sever the CICCU's links
with the nationally-respected Student Christian Movement. Their firmness
led within ten years to the birth of the IVF in 1928 [now UCCF], and to the
founding of its publishing house, IVP, in 1936. IVP would become the UK's

## GUARDING EDINBURGH'S INTENDED LEGACY

While the World Council of Churches, constituted in 1948, traces its roots back to Edinburgh 1910, there is a sense in which Lausanne is the 'spiritual legacy' of that conference, taking forward John Mott's true aspirations.

In Lausanne 1974, clear action was taken in the formation of the Programme to reclaim what had been intended. This can be seen in the strength of the speaker list,[54] and also in John Stott's first plenary address, on 'The biblical basis of evangelism'. Thirty-five years later, in 2009, the matter was still clearly on Stott's mind. Doug Birdsall and Lindsay Brown conferred with him on several occasions as the Congress was being planned. He said he felt ashamed that leaders in his own communion had refused to discuss doctrinal issues for fear of division. It had rendered John Mott's rallying cry as delegates left Edinburgh severely weakened. 'You cannot speak of the gospel of Christ and the mission of the church without reflecting on biblical truth,' he said.

Lindsay Brown's Closing Address in Cape Town would leave no doubt about the clarity of vision and

---

leading independent evangelical publisher until the early years of the 21st century. Through the endeavours of evangelical graduates in Europe and beyond, it gave rise to sister publishers in over 30 nations, with a distribution covering much of the world. The founding of Tyndale House, Cambridge in 1944 is another direct outcome of the 1919 resolve. Under God, we now see evangelicals teaching in university theology faculties and departments across the UK and around the world. A further part of the 1919 CICCU legacy was the forming in 1947 of IFES, now serving evangelical student ministries in over 160 nations.

54. See p65.

hope for Lausanne.[55] The Congress was to sound 'a ringing re-affirmation of the uniqueness of Christ and the truth of the biblical gospel and a crystal clear statement on the mission of the church - all rooted in Scripture.' To launch a movement without biblical consensus was, he said, 'folly'. The Cape Town Commitment drew evangelicals together around its biblical indicatives before moving on to its gospel imperatives. Chris Wright engaged with John Stott on the way those biblical indicatives should be crafted.[56] But let us not rush ahead.

## 1974 A CONGRESS AND A COVENANT

John Stott's reputation for clear theological thinking, his breadth of sympathy within the evangelical tradition,[57] and his gracious dealings with those of different persuasions, made him an obvious first choice to lead the process of crafting *The Lausanne Covenant*.

*The Lausanne Covenant*, which reflected the voices of the 1974 Congress, was adopted as a basis for hundreds of collaborative ventures over the rest of the century, and came to be regarded as one of the most significant documents in modern church

55. This appears in full in *The Lausanne Legacy: Landmarks in Global Mission*, Ed J E M Cameron (Hendrickson / Lausanne, 2016) pp163-172.

56. Part I of *The Cape Town Commitment*, entitled 'The Cape Town Confession of Faith', is formed around a response to God's covenantal love.

57. This evangelical 'breadth within boundaries' continues to be a value of Lausanne. In Part I of *The Cape Town Commitment* the boundaries are clearly defined.

history.[58] Social justice, too-long wrongly identified as a concern only for adherents to 'a social gospel', was now declared a biblical responsibility for evangelical Christians. This proved a watershed moment for the church. Realizing the seriousness of *The Lausanne Covenant*, John Stott worked on an exposition and commentary,

> *SOCIAL JUSTICE, WAS NOW DECLARED A BIBLICAL RESPONSIBILITY*

published in 1975. It would, he sensed, be critical for the *Covenant* to be read and studied by individuals and groups.[59] His Preface, modestly written, does not record the intense pressure of working through nights to ensure all comments received from the participants were given proper consideration. It was a mammoth operation, and first meant translating many of them into English; this was vital for the voices of the whole evangelical church to be heard.

The name 'Covenant' was carefully chosen. This was a covenant made before God himself, a covenant made between all those who wanted to adopt it. The banner on the stage, in six languages, had proclaimed 'Let the

---

58. You can listen to John Stott's presentation of *The Covenant* on the last full day of the 1974 Congress at *lausanne.org*. He and his drafting team of Samuel Escobar and Hudson Armerding, assisted by J D Douglas and Leighton Ford, invited comments at each stage of the process. They received hundreds, which were all carefully considered. It was a finely-tuned and meticulous process. *The Covenant* truly reflected the voices and mood of the Congress.

59. Now in *The Lausanne Legacy*, pp13-53.

Earth hear His Voice'; for that to happen, the whole evangelical church needed to work together.

'*The Lausanne Covenant* was 'prophetic', wrote Chris Wright, 'in the sense of speaking in a way which applied the word of God to the realities of the hour. And it retains its relevance and challenge now, and indeed for generations to come.' He continued, 'May its creative combinations of confidence and humility, of human energy and trust in God, of vision and realism, of joy in the Lord's doings and grief over our human failures, of strategic thinking and the Spirit's leading, of global vision and local action, of words and works – always remain characteristic of the Lausanne Movement, as they are of its *Covenant*.[60]

In July 1989 John Stott led the crafting team for *The Manila Manifesto* in the Second Lausanne Congress (Manila, Philippines), which in 31 Clauses built on and elaborated *The Lausanne Covenant*. This Congress took place a month after what the Chinese government termed the 'Tiananmen Incident', and just three months before the dismantling of the Berlin Wall. It drew 3,000 participants from 170 countries including Eastern Europe and the Soviet Union, but sadly none from China. Lausanne II in Manila [as it became known] was the catalyst for over 300 partnerships and new initiatives, in the developing world and elsewhere.

Five years before Lausanne II, John Stott completed his new and groundbreaking book Issues *Facing*

60. See Foreword to 2008 edition included in *The Lausanne Legacy*, pp10-12.

*Christians Today*. This was a major contribution to evangelical thinking. It covered nuclear issues, pluralism, human rights, industrialization, sexual issues... It became a handbook for pastors and thinking church members, It was, he said, his 'contribution to the catching-up process' since the church was 'recovering from its temporarily-mislaid social conscience'. *The Lausanne Covenant* was continuing to create waves, reawakening a social conscience which had lain dormant in many quarters for perhaps two generations. The Lord Jesus had commissioned the apostles to teach new disciples 'everything' he had commanded them. This had plainly not been done. In God's grace, John Stott and the Lausanne Movement would become a means of re-establishing significant aspects of Christian duty.

## FORMING A MOVEMENT FROM A CONGRESS

After the 1974 Congress, a Continuation Committee was set up, to build on what had been achieved. In January 1975 this group met in Mexico City with Bishop Jack Dain in the chair. There was considerable support for Billy Graham to become President of the new Lausanne Committee for World Evangelization, as it was then named. John Stott urged that this not be allowed to happen, or that there be several Co-Presidents. Billy Graham had already articulated his preference that the Movement adopt a narrower brief of what we could call Proclamation evangelism. If this were followed, the

Movement would reflect neither the scriptural mandate of the church to be salt and light, nor its own historical roots. On the strength of their 20-year friendship, John

## JOHN STOTT, THOUGH HATING DISCORD, FELT THE NEED TO SPEAK

Stott, though hating discord, felt the need to speak. Jack Dain was in agreement, while others could not bring themselves to voice anything other than blind allegiance to Billy Graham, given his worldwide stature.

Some perceived it as a power struggle. Billy Graham saw his mistake in yielding to the pressure to accept the role. John Stott was asked to be on the drafting committee to prepare a statement on the progress of the meetings, a statement which was accepted with only minor amendments. He described this in his diary as 'a helpful note of unanimity on which to conclude a rather traumatic conference.'[61]

When the Continuation Committee met the following year in Atlanta, four separate functions were identified as being needed to achieve the Movement's aims: (i) Intercession (ii) Theology and Education (iii) Strategy (iv) Communication. A working group for each was set up, and all four of these groups remain now. John Stott became Chairman of the Theology and

---

61. See full story in *A Global Ministry*, Chapter 7. John Stott always maintained that evangelism must be primary, but that a need to make a choice between evangelism and social justice was really very rare. Following the Cape Town Congress, Blair Carlson was appointed to a newly-created Lausanne role of Ambassador for Proclamation Evangelism.

Education Working Group (later called the Theology Working Group).

As a backdrop to his preparation of *Issues*, John continued to make Lausanne consultations a priority. Not only was he there, but frequently in the Chair. He edited the papers from all the consultations up to Lausanne II under the title *Making Christ Known*. As is clear from the contributors, Lausanne had the standing (helped, no doubt by John's own presence) to draw the best evangelical thinkers globally.

*Making Christ Known*[62] opened with *The Lausanne Covenant* (1974) and finished with *The Manila Manifesto* (1989). Some papers such as the 1977 *Pasadena Statement on the Homogeneous Unit Principle* [ie of church growth and evangelization], and the 1980 *Evangelical Commitment to Simple Lifestyle* gained considerable traction. All are still available online as *Lausanne Occasional Papers*, and each carries the names of the invited participants; formidable lists of their day. As John surveyed his years in Lausanne, he looked forward with anticipation to what Cape Town 2010 would bring.

## ITS FRUIT 'GROWS ON OTHER PEOPLE'S TREES'

For as long as the Lausanne Movement was characterized by 'the spirit of Lausanne' John Stott sensed it was critically placed. Humility would always be needful. It is said of Lausanne that its fruit

---

62. See footnote 2 for publishing details.

'grows on other people's trees'. It has always acted most effectively as a catalyst. Its platform has drawn and draws from across the divides of secondary issues, incorporating the evangelical church in its widest sense – including, for example, specialized mission agencies which bring focused knowledge; Christians in the public arenas of Government, Business, Academia who shake salt and shine light; believers in nominally Christian cultures; minority Christian groups under oppressive regimes; rich and poor...

Through consultations, as leaders meet face-to-face and get to know one another as friends, John Stott sensed that Lausanne would offer a unique means for the church to share the gifts Christ gives.

## PASTOR-THEOLOGIAN

John Stott was one of the few true pastor-theologians. People mattered. We cannot strategize with integrity about world evangelization if we do not care about the people in our own town. John Stott was an integrated man. While a schoolboy at Rugby, he had founded the ABC Club as a way to provide a bath for vagrants. As a curate, he had taken boys from the poorer families in the parish for their first experience of camping. As a rector, he sometimes gave up his bed to homeless men, and slept on a camp bed in his study.

The term 'glocal' which was coined in the 1990s in the context of fast-moving globalization, describes the way John Stott had lived consistently since the

1930s. It was a core value for him. As one of the world's most effective global public evangelists, he cared for individuals locally, whatever their status. While Lausanne would always function at a strategic level, among

**'GLOCAL' WAS A CORE VALUE FOR HIM**

theological thinkers, it would be of no more worth than a resounding gong or clanging cymbal if the benefit of its networking did not touch down in real life situations.

## SETTING ASPIRATIONS FOR LAUSANNE

John Stott's gifts as an expositor, a writer, and a thinker with wide intellectual reach were combined with a natural humility. His aspirations for the church fitted precisely with Billy Graham's aspirations for the 1974 Congress. His name had already become synonymous with the diligent handling of scripture, and with a doctrine of scripture as a touchstone for all human experience and enterprise. This lent significant strength to Lausanne's standing.

Invitations to speak at the 1974 Congress included some of the most able evangelical thinkers: Francis Schaeffer, Samuel Escobar, Jim Packer, Henri Blocher, the young Os Guinness, and the recent convert Malcolm Muggeridge. Stott's seminal address on the biblical basis for evangelism opened with the dialogue on meaning between Alice-in-Wonderland and Humpty Dumpty. Very English. Very simple. Very memorable.

Why go for high-sounding philosophy or philology, when a story written for a seven-year-old will work?

At Lausanne II in Manila in 1989, he gave the first three expositions, covering Romans 1-5, on 'Eagerness to preach the gospel', 'The world's guilt' and 'Amazing Grace'. He loved any chance to help people into the Pauline epistles. Friends said that, like the Apostle Paul, he was 'obsessed by the cross'.

## THE THIRD LAUSANNE CONGRESS: CAPE TOWN 2010

John Stott and Billy Graham both sent greetings to the Third Lausanne Congress. John would have loved to be there, and briefly considered the possibility, despite his advancing frailty. He wrote:

'I shall be very sorry to miss being with you in Cape Town. But I will be with you all each day in prayer, expectation and confidence as you plan to make known the uniqueness of Jesus Christ all over the world.'[63]

In March 2011 he received a copy of *The Cape Town Commitment*, and asked friends to read it to him, as his eyesight had faded. Each of the ministries and endeavours with which John Stott had been closely associated was part of The Third Lausanne Congress. All the matters in which he had yearned for evangelicals to

---

63. Then, following a reflection on Lausanne since 1974, the growth of the Church, and his particular delight that the Congress was being hosted in Africa, he concluded: 'As you will be studying Ephesians together, my encouragement to you echoes the Apostle Paul. 'I urge you to live a life worthy of the calling you have received. Be completely humble and gentle; be patient, bearing with one another in love. Make every effort to keep the unity of the Spirit in the bond of peace.'

engage were clearly laid out – not just in a document, but in a *commitment*, firmly rooted in a response to God's covenantal love. He knew of the unhurried process which had taken place, before and during the Congress, to listen to the voices of evangelical leaders from across the world; to discern what the Holy Spirit is saying to the church, in terms of priorities.

John Stott had heard of plans being laid for global consultations to take forward the major areas in *The Cape Town Commitment*. It built on his huge efforts in Lausanne and Manila. No doubt there was a sense of completion as he listened to it being read.

*Julia Cameron, Director of Communications for the Third Lausanne Congress, then to 2019 Lausanne Director of Publishing. Founder of Dictum, and honorary Director of Publishing for EFAC.*

# A VISION FOR WHOLE-LIFE DISCIPLESHIP

**Mark Greene**

John was 61 years old when the London Institute for Contemporary Christianity (LICC) was founded. At that point in his life he could instead have pastored a church, or taught in almost any seminary or theological college in the world. He could have concentrated only on his global itinerant preaching and teaching ministry, or accepted an episcopal call, with a seat in the House of Lords. But instead he chose to focus much energy around this new, small institute for contemporary Christianity

*EVANGELICAL PREACHING WAS BESET BY THE SACRED-SECULAR DIVIDE*

John and a few friends[64] saw with searing clarity how hard evangelicals found it to apply the word of God to issues we encounter. Evangelical preaching was beset by the sacred-secular divide, which left pastors and lay people with a narrow concept of mission, and a narrow vision for discipleship

---

64. Several friends had significant input into the vision for LICC, including Oliver Barclay, Brian Griffiths, Jim Houston and Os Guinness. Then John Stott and Andrew Kirk worked together to hone the vision. LICC opened its doors in 1982.

and disciple-making. One of John's major contributions to this area, shortly after the London Institute was founded, is his book *Issues Facing Christians Today*.[65]

The LICC faculty gave lectures on the hot topics of the era, and sought to engage with pressing concerns.[66] At the heart of LICC was 'whole-life discipleship'. Its unique ten-week residential course, 'The Christian in the Modern World' (CMW), combined listening to the word and the world: understanding culture, mission and discipleship.

> *THE LICC FACULTY GAVE LECTURES ON THE HOT TOPICS OF THE ERA*

The CMW course brought together Christians from a whole variety of walks of life, and from every continent – lawyers, doctors, business people, pastors, cross-cultural missionaries, para-church workers. The result was a wonderfully vibrant mix of people who were helped to think outside the confines of their own culture. Together they were compelled to recognize that the Bible needed to be applied beyond the church and their local culture, to every sphere of life. Today, you can see the fruit of that course in the lives of its alumni, who have gone

---

65. First published in 1982 (Marshall, Morgan and Scott), now by HarperCollins, and regularly updated.

66. For example Martyn Eden (social and political issues), Ernest Lucas (science), Andrew Kirk (Global South), Elaine Storkey (gender issues). The Institute's 'Offspring' project saw day conferences take place around the country. These led to several local 'Schools of Christian Studies' in UK towns and cities.

on to make a significant impact for Christ. Some have founded variations of LICC in their own countries.

John was one of the greatest preachers of his

*HE NEVER ELEVATED THAT CALLING ABOVE ANY OTHER*

generation, but he never elevated that calling above any other. He was interested in raising up a new generation of missional Christian disciples in every area of life, not just a new generation of preachers.

He taught and wrote and preached at All Souls and all round the world, and he also discipled. Most of his study assistants, disciples by any other name, pursued a preaching and teaching ministry. But John saw discipling in a much wider context. For example he met with a group of business people in London for a regular prayer breakfast. And he met with young professionals in diverse fields to engage biblically with key books, films, exhibitions, events. He listened carefully to everyone but, as one of them put it, 'he was really teaching us to engage with culture.'

John was essentially a disciple-maker. He was making disciples for ministry in the church, for ministry in business, for ministry in every area of life. This is a goal and a practice that very few church leaders have emulated. The inseparability of proclaiming the gospel and practically pursuing social justice[67] has now been

67. As brought together in Section 5, 'The Lausanne Covenant'. See *The Lausanne Legacy*, p28.

grasped in principle by large sections of the global evangelical church. But there is more work to do in helping to equip the laity for whole-life mission and whole-life discipleship.

The mission strategy of most churches is focused around people using leisure time to join missionary initiatives led by church-paid workers. This vital part of the mission of God has borne much fruit, but is only one part of the whole.

John recruited a rich mix of people to come to LICC for the CMW course. He taught double-listening: listening to the word and listening to the world. But the course actually engaged in triple listening: listening to the word, listening to the world, and listening to one

*THE COURSE ACTUALLY ENGAGED IN TRIPLE LISTENING*

another in humility, seeking to help one another fulfil our diverse callings, individual and corporate, in the diverse settings where God has placed us. A teacher, lawyer or a mechanic should go to work with a sense of representing the body of Christ, supported in prayer and fellowship, and able to draw on the wisdom of a local body of believers, to the glory of the Father.

It was a radical vision back in 1982, and it still is. LICC's team is now much larger and our range of activity broader, but the focus remains the same as that of our founders – namely envisioning and equipping God's people, lay and ordained, for whole-life mission. Our website shows our resources – print, digital, events – and our work in advocacy. Will you join us?

*Mark Greene, Executive Director of the London Institute for Contemporary Christianity, is former Vice Principal of the London School of Theology. After graduating from Cambridge, he spent ten years in the advertising industry in London and New York.*

# JOHN STOTT AND A ROCHA

## Dave Bookless

John Stott's birdwatching was legendary. Wherever he travelled he would have his binoculars and, if possible, his camera and a guidebook to the region's birds. He would plan time around his speaking engagements to slip away, often taking others whom he sought to introduce to his passion for 'orni-theology', a term he most-likely invented. He kept rigorous lists and notes of his bird observations from childhood onwards, and saw 2,500-3,000 species in his travels to many countries.[68]

Some have assumed Uncle John's birding to be a harmless eccentricity and a diversion from his Kingdom work, and have similarly dismissed A Rocha[69] as a peculiar anomaly for Christian birdwatchers. Yet, this fails to understand the profound scope of John's discipleship, the integration of his faith and all of his life, and why he was deeply involved with A Rocha from its beginnings until his death. In *John Stott: A portrait by his friends*, Peter Harris, who founded A Rocha with his wife Miranda, described John as 'probably more

---

68. Miranda Harris, (2013) https://tinyurl.com/yb3zo7bm

69. Portuguese for 'the rock'. Sometimes seen in print as 'Arocha'.

profoundly converted than anyone else I have known.'[70] For John, meditating on God's revelation in creation and taking practical action to conserve God's world,

*JOHN WAS 'PROBABLY MORE PROFOUNDLY CONVERTED THAN ANYONE ELSE I HAVE KNOWN*

were both theologically driven by obedience to scripture. He was only half joking when he pointed out, frequently, that Jesus used the imperative tense in telling his followers to 'look at the birds of the air' (Matthew 6:26).[71] Actually, according to his own account, John's passion for birdwatching happened almost by accident when, as a child, his precious collection of butterflies and moths was accidentally destroyed by his sister. It was his father who diverted the attention of the inconsolable young boy onto birds.[72]

John Stott's links with A Rocha began with a very personal connection to its founders, Peter and Miranda Harris. Peter wrote to John in 1982 when planning a UCCF (Intervarsity) expedition to Falsterbo Bird Observatory in Sweden. Some leaders in the Christian student movement needed convincing this was an appropriate activity, and John happily gave it his

---

70. In *John Stott: A Portrait by his Friends*. Ed: Chris Wright (IVP, 2011) p156.

71. For example, see *Under the Bright Wings* by Peter Harris (Hodder & Stoughton, 1993) p120.

72. See *John Stott and The Hookses* by David Cranston (Words by Design, 2017), p14.

blessing, writing to Peter 'I wish I could have joined you!'[73] Peter shared his vision of establishing 'a Christian field study centre and bird observatory' in Portugal, and asked if John

## HOW OFTEN DID JOHN USE TWO EXCLAMATION MARKS?

would be prepared to join its Council of Reference. John's reply was typical. He would refuse unless he could be involved personally, asking Peter to visit him in London, and adding 'perhaps also I should insist on your inviting me to visit ... Portugal at the earliest moment!!'[74] How often did John use two exclamation marks?

The beginnings of A Rocha in Portugal in 1983 coincided with John's first serious theological foray into environmental issues. In *Issues Facing Christians Today*, published in 1984, he included a chapter on 'The Human Environment'. He explored reasons for concern, listing population growth, resource depletion and runaway technology (and, in a later edition, climate change), quoting from the most authoritative sources at the time. He went on to explain a biblical perspective on creation care. The earth belongs to God by creation, to us by delegation, he wrote, and 'our possession of the earth, therefore, is leasehold not freehold.'[75]

---

73. Letter from John Stott to Peter Harris, 20 December 1982.

74. Ibid.

75. *Issues Facing Christians Today* p111.

He went on to explain that scripture is clear about humanity's dominion over creation, but this should be understood as both 'cooperative', in that we are to work with, not against, natural processes, and also 'a delegated, and therefore a responsible, dominion'.[76]

As A Rocha became established during the 1980s, John Stott kept closely in touch. On visiting Portugal in 1985, Miranda Harris recalled meeting him for the first time: 'Dashing through the front door of our rented Portuguese house, desperately trying to avoid some looming crisis in the kitchen, I thrust our three-week-old baby into the arms of a white-haired stranger in a light blue suit, standing in the shadowy hallway. Returning a few moments later I found John gently rocking her, tutting in a soothing way, and we introduced ourselves. Thus began twenty five years of friendship with our family.'[77] The friendship was genuine and mutual, with John enjoying getting to know the Harris children as well as their parents. When Peter wrote the remarkable story of A Rocha's beginnings in *Under the Bright Wings*, John Stott wrote in the Foreword, 'It will be evident to readers that I love and admire Peter and Miranda … I thank God for their vision, commitment, faith and perseverance, their love for the people they are seeking to serve, and their deep immersion in the Portuguese language and culture. In the developing ministry of A Rocha an exciting,

---

76. *Issues*, p114.

77. Miranda Harris (2013) https://tinyurl.com/y77n5mma

contemporary form of Christian mission has come alive.'[78]

*AN EXCITING, CONTEMPORARY FORM OF CHRISTIAN MISSION HAS COME ALIVE*

Over the coming years, John joined Peter on a number of birding expeditions. Where possible, Miranda came too, often accompanied by other A Rocha team members, helping John to get to know the growing movement of Christians in conservation. In 1989 they visited Portugal, Gibraltar and Morocco. In 1992 it was north west Turkey, in 1994 Spain, and later on there were A Rocha-linked birding visits in the US, Romania, Syria and Lebanon, Ethiopia and Kenya, and the UK. For John, as for the A Rocha folk, these were not just holidays. They were times of refreshment and renewal, and opportunities to know God's creation better, and through that the God behind it. Often John would bring his latest writing project with him. Miranda shared vivid memories of the Turkish visit, when John was writing his commentary on Romans. The others got up for some early morning birding, only to find John 'emerging from his room around 6.30 am after two hours of study, slightly shining – rather like Moses coming down from the mountain.'[79]

We read in the Gospels that Jesus took himself off to a quiet place to pray (Mark 1:35). Similarly, for John, spending time in the wild beauty of creation deepened

---

78. John Stott in *Under the Bright Wings*, p xi.

79. Miranda Harris (2013) https://tinyurl.com/ycxswyxn

his fellowship with the Father and prepared him for busy times of ministry. He once wrote, 'Birding takes

## BIRDING TRANSPLANTS YOU INTO THE TRANQUILLITY OF THE WILDERNESS

your mind off everything. It rescues you from the noise, the bustle and the pressures of city life, and transplants you into the tranquillity of the wilderness. Few experiences are more healing to the spirit than rising with the sun and wandering out ... if possible with a friend, but otherwise alone with the sights, the sounds and the smells of nature, and with the living God, who conceived and contrived it all.'[80] Although he disliked the term 'spirituality' for its connotations of relativistic, pick-and-mix religion, it can be said that John Stott had an authentically biblical creation spirituality. He often preached on the Psalms, which so eloquently evoke creation's worship as coming before and often beyond human worship.

John Stott's involvement in A Rocha was far more than light birding relief from his exhausting global responsibilities; more even than personal friendship with the Harris family, although both those mattered to him. He was also engaged strategically, with typically rigorous biblical insight, in articulating how A Rocha's work in community-based biodiversity conservation fitted into a biblical worldview. He spoke both at A Rocha's 10th anniversary celebrations, held at St Paul's,

---

80. *John Stott and the Hookses*, p15.

Robert Adam Street in 1993, and at the 20th anniversary gathering in Ferragudo, Portugal, in 2003. The decade between saw astonishing growth from a single project in Portugal to, ten years later, further projects in Bulgaria, Canada, Czech Republic, Finland, France, Ghana, India, Kenya, Lebanon, Netherlands, the UK and the USA, along with prospective ones in Peru and South Africa.

I was at both these gatherings and was deeply challenged and informed by John Stott's talks. In 1993, he spoke on 'The Works of the Lord', based on Psalms 103 and 104 as companion Psalms, reminding us of God's great 'works' in creation and in salvation, and that both should be the subject of our study, our worship and our witness.[81] Barbara Mearns, who became A Rocha's administrator, said later, 'This sermon was one of the most memorable and encouraging and empowering I have ever heard. I had never heard a minister preach on God as Creator before, not like John did.'[82] In the same year, he wrote 'Can ecological involvement be properly included under the heading of 'mission'? Yes, it can and should. For mission embraces everything Christ sends his people into the world to do, service as well as evangelism. ... The gospel itself includes God's creation as well as his work of redemption.'[83]

---

81. *The Works of the Lord* by John Stott (A Rocha Trust privately published leaflet, 1983).

82. Barbara Mearns, from a personal email.

83. John Stott in *Under the Bright Wings*, p x.

As A Rocha's ministry grew, and new projects began in various countries, John was called on to help in multiple ways. He crafted the wording for what

*HE CRAFTED THE WORDING FOR WHAT BECAME 'THE 5Cs'*

became 'A Rocha's Five Core Commitments', or simply 'The 5Cs', defining it as a movement that was firstly deeply Christian, secondly doing practical Conservation, working in and with Community, intentionally Cross-cultural, and committed to Co-operation.[84] In 1997 he spoke in Beirut at a launch conference for A Rocha Lebanon, at the start of Chris and Susanna Naylor's remarkable pioneering work in achieving the transformation of the Aammiq Wetland in the Bekaa Valley.[85] It was the largest gathering of Christian leaders in war-torn Lebanon for over 20 years, and John's reputation meant they listened and responded as he talked of caring for creation as intrinsic to the gospel. Miranda Harris wrote later, 'His early endorsement of A Rocha through this event paved the way to good relationships with Christian leaders which the Naylors could build on.'[86]

He also spoke at a similar launch conference in Nairobi for A Rocha Kenya, preached for an A Rocha

---

84. https://www.arocha.org/en/values

85. The story is beautifully told in Postcards from the Middle East by Chris Naylor (Lion Publishing, 2015).

86. Miranda Harris (2013) https://tinyurl.com/ycmmn23c

service at the British Birdwatching Fair and, when A Rocha UK began in 2001, he visited the Minet site, wrote personal letters of support, and invited the team to come to his Welsh writing retreat, The Hookses, to spend a week with him there in both 2005 and 2006. These were vital times of strategic planning as well as spiritual retreat, and John's wisdom, encouragement and gentle humour were crucial. Even though his eyesight and energy were waning, John was in his element in the place where so much of his writing was done, where he had once spoken of sitting in his favourite spot, before a forthcoming major mission, watching the wheeling Choughs and diving Gannets: 'Here on my secret cliff-ledge I sat and thought and prayed and prepared and, I believe, met with the living God until my heart's fears were largely pacified.'[87]

> HERE ON MY SECRET CLIFF-LEDGE I MET WITH THE LIVING GOD

In 2007, A Rocha made a short film, for which John agreed to be recorded at The Hookses. With the Pembrokeshire coast behind him, he stated: 'For over 20 years I have been an enthusiastic supporter of A Rocha, and I take this opportunity to commend to you their practical and educational work around the world. They are, in my judgment, a very fine organization which is worthy of our support.'[88] When his final book, *The*

87. *John Stott and The Hookses*, p18.

88. Video at https://tinyurl.com/y9rbfnlm

*Radical Disciple*, was published in 2010, John urged his readers to 'consider eight characteristics of Christian discipleship which are often neglected and yet deserve

'CREATION-
CARE IS AN
INCREASINGLY
MAINLINE
CHRISTIAN
CONCERN'

to be taken seriously'.[89] Fourth in his list was 'Creation-Care' where he recalled speaking at the A Rocha Kenya launch conference and emphasised that 'creation-care is neither a selfish interest of the developed 'north', nor a minority enthusiasm peculiar to birdwatchers or flower-lovers, but an increasingly mainline Christian concern.'[90]

Today, A Rocha continues to see John's vision of 'creation care as an increasingly mainline Christian concern', come to fruition. In October 2019 a terrible car accident in South Africa killed Chris and Susanna Naylor and Miranda Harris, also severely injuring Peter Harris[91]. The loss to their families, to A Rocha globally, and to the worldwide creation care movement, is severe and heart-breaking. Yet, and this is tribute to the Harrises and Naylors as well as to John Stott's writing and advocacy over many years, A Rocha now has such a broad base of support and recognition across six continents that its work is continuing and

---

89. *The Radical Disciple* by John Stott (IVP, 2010) p17.

90. Ibid, p57.

91. https://www.arocha.org/en/news/a-rocha-in-mourning-over-loss-of-three-leaders/

developing despite this devastating setback. Perhaps, at last, the global church is recognising that, in John's words, 'It is a noble calling to cooperate with God for the fulfilment of his purposes. In this way our work is to be an expression of our worship since our care of the creation will reflect our love for the Creator.'[92]

*Revd Dr Dave Bookless is Director of Theology for A Rocha International, and Lausanne Global Catalyst for Creation Care. Dave writes on, and travels widely to speak on, creation care.*

---

92. *The Radical Disciple* p59.

The Snowy Owl. This photo was the crown of a 25-year search by John Stott. Now, having found his quarry, he said (with some rather Anglican humour) that he felt he could 'sing the Nunc Dimittis'. See *The Birds our Teachers* for the story.

The landmark pillars and spire of All Souls, designed by John Nash (1824). Before traffic built up, John Stott could hear the 'rasping song' of the Black Redstart, perched on top of Broadcasting House (next door), as he offered Holy Communion in the early service.

# PART IV

# VOICES FROM AROUND THE WORLD

# DAILY BIBLE READING

**Las Newman**

When I was a young theological student in Canada, in the late 1970s, I had the privilege of serving as Uncle John's student aide when he conducted a mission at the University of Toronto. On the last day of the mission he asked me if I was acquainted with Robert Murray McCheyne's Bible reading plan. I told him I wasn't.

He said, 'My dear Las, this plan will change your knowledge and grasp of the Bible as a whole.' He handed me a copy, and it has helped me on my journey through the Bible ever since. I found out afterwards that Dr Martyn Lloyd-Jones had, in the 1950s, handed a copy to Uncle John in just the same way, and that John had used it for the rest of his life. The McCheyne reading plan has long been the most widely-used reading plan in the world, but it was first designed by McCheyne for the congregation he pastored in St Peter's Free Church, Dundee, Scotland. It was, to quote what McCheyne wrote to his congregation, 'to be a helper of [their] joy.'

John Stott wrote some years later: 'To me its great value is that it begins with the four 'great beginnings' in Scripture – Genesis (the birth of the universe), Ezra (the rebirth of the nation after Babylonian captivity),

Matthew (the birth of Christ) and Acts (the birth of the body of Christ). Then we follow the unfolding of these four stories.' He finished, 'Nothing has helped me more than this to grasp the grand themes of the Bible.'

Using McCheyne has helped me to balance my devotional and theological reading of the Old and New Testaments in a consistent way. As it was commended to me, so I highly commend it to others.[93]

*Dr Las G Newman, former IFES Associate General Secretary, then President of the Caribbean Graduate School of Theology, is a Global Associate Director of the Lausanne Movement.*

---

93. Available as a free download. Also published in print with a short Introduction by John Stott (Dictum / EFAC).

# JOHN STOTT AS A MODEL OF BIBLICAL VALUES

### Ajith Fernando

John Stott became a mentor while I was still a university student, long before I met him, through books borrowed from my layman father's library. I first read his addresses to the Urbana Missions Conventions, and his exposition of Romans 5-8: *Men Made New*. Later there came a long list of books, especially the *Bible Speaks Today* series, which

> *JOHN STOTT BECAME A MENTOR LONG BEFORE I MET HIM*

modelled Bible exposition for us younger preachers. One of his greatest contributions to the church, in my view, was the way he demonstrated the glory of Bible exposition.

I met John Stott personally for the first time while a student at Fuller Seminary in the mid-1970s. I went to every talk on the programme in his one-day visit. During a Question and Answer session, a student asked him about study habits. In an earlier era, he said, pastors spent the whole morning studying, but that was impractical now. Instead, we should squeeze in whatever time we could find during the day to study. Squeezing in study time became an ambition in my life. The next time I met Stott was in Singapore, when he spoke at the Lausanne Movement's Asian Leadership Conference on Evangelism (ALCOE, 1978). The first thing he asked me was, 'Are you finding time to study?'

At this conference someone asked about contextualization, which was just becoming a buzz word. Stott's response surprised us. Contextualization,

## WE SHOULD KNOW OUR SOCIETY, AND APPLY THE BIBLE IN IT

he said, began with studying the Bible, and knowing it deeply. Then, he said, we should know our society, and apply the Bible in it. This was what came to be known as 'double listening'. His

writing on key topics became definitive treatments. They were first and foremost biblical, and they applied biblical truth to contemporary society. They showed how biblical truth should be practised, and they engaged with controversial issues; another great contribution to the church.

*I Believe in Preaching* (1982)[94] set a new standard for preaching. We are representatives of the great God in this world and must work hard at buttressing the presentation of God's truth with both accuracy and relevance. Then came *Issues Facing Christians Today* (1984) which looked at social and ethical issues, and went into several editions. My favourite is *The Cross of Christ* (1986), the most enriching theological book I have read. It is one of the few books on the cross which

---

94. US title *Between Two Worlds*, also 1982.

addresses questions non-Christians ask about the
death of Christ.

For about four months I took *The Cross of Christ*
with me wherever I went. I wrote copious notes in the
margins, composed a detailed table of contents, and
compiled my own topical index at the back. Once I was
travelling home by bus from a camp in the mountains.
It was a six-hour journey, and I had to stand as the bus
was full, so could not read while the bus was moving.
I read while I waited for the bus, and then reached
for the book again from a rack above the seats each
time the bus stopped to drop and pick up passengers.
Suddenly someone said that a book had fallen out of
the bus through the window. I knew it was my precious
book, and took my bag and got off the bus to go in
search of it. People on the road informed me that
someone in a bus coming the other way had seen it
fall, stopped their bus, and picked it up.

As they explained this, a
police jeep arrived. The police
asked what had happened and,
when they heard, let me get into
the jeep, and we gave chase

*POLICE LET ME GET INTO THE JEEP, AND WE GAVE CHASE*

after the bus! We finally caught it up in the next town. I
gratefully took possession of the book and proceeded
on my journey. This was a book I could not afford to
lose, with all its notes.

For Christians in Asia, the measures of effective
leadership can bear the trappings of earthly success

– a huge audience, a luxurious house, an expensive car. A speaker may bring a large entourage and breeze in with a huge car or even by helicopter. He may have little personal contact with people. Stott was just the opposite, and even the secular media recognised this humble man as one of the most influential people of the twentieth century.[95] He lived out servanthood to a bewildered generation of emerging Christians leaders.

## HE LIVED OUT SERVANTHOOD TO EMERGING LEADERS

My first visit to John Stott's home in London left a deep impression on me. Among the things in that spartan flat was a kneeler, where he prayed. One of the first questions he asked me was 'How is Jeyaraj?' Jeyaraj is a Youth for Christ staffworker in Sri Lanka, who was wrongly arrested on suspicion of terrorism, then released after fifteen months, without any charges laid against him. He had an amazing ministry in prison. I had asked prayer for Jeyaraj in my six-monthly newsletter. Stott had not only been praying for him, but he also remembered his difficult name! Here he emulated Paul who prayed for a large number of people in different parts of the Christian world. A wide and large prayer list goes with being a servant of the global Church.

John Stott did not join those who used e-mail as their primary means of communication. Through a wide

95. For example *TIME* magazine, April 2005, where he is listed as one of the 100 most influential people in the world; and the substantial space given to his obituaries in the UK broadsheets and other media.

personal correspondence, he showed active concern for individuals. What a surprise it was for this 34-year-old unknown preacher to receive a copy of his book *I Believe in Preaching* personally inscribed, 'Ajith – friend and brother in the gospel of Christ, with esteem and affection. John Stott.' In later correspondence he called himself 'Uncle John'. His annual newsletter always included a personal note to me and my wife whom he mentioned by name, until it became too difficult for him to write personal notes. He would often respond to my six-monthly newsletter with a handwritten letter on an aerogramme. If I had mentioned a book I was hoping to write, he would send titles of books that would help me in preparing.

> *HE WOULD SEND TITLES OF BOOKS THAT WOULD HELP ME*

My friend Dr Peter Kuzmic once went to an airport chapel to pray. He saw the grey head of a man in the front of the chapel, arranging papers. It was John Stott, sorting through hundreds of letters. His published output alone was enormous. But he also wrote personal letters to hundreds of younger leaders, to encourage and instruct. Inspired by this I decided that if I am to have an international ministry, I too will need to spend considerable time in writing letters.

The Lausanne Younger Leaders' Conference in Singapore in 1987 was a defining moment in many leaders' lives. I was on the organizing committee. John Stott expressed his desire to be there to encourage those attending. Most of the speakers were themselves younger leaders. We were happy to hear that he was coming, but could allot him only one talk. To me this seemed an embarrassing act of disrespect to an elder

*HE STAYED FOR ALL TEN DAYS, JUST TO ENCOURAGE US*

statesman. But he became the hero of the conference by *not* speaking! He stayed for all ten days, just to be an encouragement to us. Finding a quiet corner on the university campus where we met, he would sit and talk with people by appointment. I was one who benefited in that way.

During the late 1980s, Lausanne's chairman, Leighton Ford, was advocating that we be Kingdom seekers rather than empire builders. Stott exemplified this in Singapore and all through his life. He left no new structures to perpetuate his influence, because he was intent on strengthening existing structures. As Chris Wright shows us, the organization which emerged from his ministry, Langham Partnership, focuses on equipping other ministries rather than building its own structures.

John Stott's international ministry coincided with the shift of the centre of gravity of Christianity to the Majority World. This has not been a smooth transition. Many Majority World leaders felt that Western leaders did not even try to understand what they were saying. They suspected them of empire building. This gave rise to an almost racist animosity among some of the sharpest minds in the Majority World church towards Western church leadership. With Westerners like John Stott, and other Lausanne leaders Leighton Ford, John Reid, Jack Dain and Robert Coleman,

*IT WAS IMPOSSIBLE TO HAVE ANGRY THOUGHTS TOWARDS WESTERNERS*

who endeavoured to be servants to our churches, it was impossible for me to have my life sullied by angry thoughts towards Westerners.

John Stott truly exemplified servanthood to the world church. At a time when evangelicals are criticized as arrogant for insisting on the finality of Christ, no apologetic is as vital as a servant lifestyle.

*Dr Ajith Fernando is former National Director, and now Teaching Director, of Sri Lanka Youth for Christ. He is widely known as an author and Bible teacher, and was a plenary expositor at the Third Lausanne Congress.*

# FRIENDSHIP, INFLUENCE AND THE FUTURE

## Nigel Cameron

John Stott's links with IFES movements around the world gave him unique access to some of the keenest up-and-coming minds, across the disciplines. He would hand-pick students and young graduates to look with him at some of the new frontiers. They included future lawyers and professors of bioethics, medicine and theology. With an eye to their later influence, he would draw them into discussions, to introduce them to academics and theologically-reflective practitioners whose credentials were already established. His vision was to equip the church to serve the nations. In this, friendship was central. Nigel Cameron explains:

'Friendship featured highly in all John Stott's ministry and dealings; he worked and he networked through friendship. This gift of friendship, combined with his interdisciplinary and enquiring mind, equipped him to bring traditional Christianity to bear on science, medicine, contemporary thinking about war and nuclear deterrence, and other such big questions. He was perhaps uniquely able to convene that largely private discussion among the upper echelons of science and medicine and the armed forces... as he laboured mightily to bridge the Christian faith community and the hottest of emerging issues.

'It struck me then [in the 1970s], and does more forcefully now, how his network of personal friendships, which snaked across the face of the planet, was both embedded in his character, and was, more than anything else, the key to his astonishing influence.'

*Prof Nigel Cameron is founder and former President of the Center for Policy on Emerging Technologies, Washington DC. This is taken from his tribute to John Stott in* The Times *(8 August 2011).*

# 'UNCLE JOHN'S PARISH EXTENDED TO FRANCOPHONE AFRICA'

## Daniel Bourdanné

John Stott loved Francophone Africa and visited several countries in the region. At a time of harsh ethnic conflict, he travelled to both Rwanda and Burundi in the Great Lakes region and brought much encouragement to believers there. As an untiring ambassador for students, he spoke with church leaders in support of the GBU, underlining the strategic nature of this movement. I remember the impact of his visit on the churches and on the GBU students.

In fact church leaders and other Christians across Francophone African have been profoundly influenced by this pastor and evangelical theologian, not least through his books. The first one I read was *L'essentiel du Christianisme [Basic Christianity]*, while a student in Togo. In our Bible study group, we were looking for books which would engage with fellow students and help us to articulate our faith. We wanted to offer our non-believing friends a book which was clear and intellectually rigorous, and which would summarise evangelical Christianity.

His short book, *Plaidoyer pour une foi intelligente [Your Mind Matters]*, helped countless students and Francophone African intellectuals to articulate their faith intelligently. Through this, John Stott made a lasting contribution. He urged us not to neglect our intellect as we live out our faith.

John Stott's views on evangelism and social action, on showing respect for cultures, on openness to dialogue, and his major work *Le chrétien et les défis de la vie moderne [Issues Facing Christians Today]* have been widely influential in Francophone Africa. Readers of his work heard an echo of a Christian faith which fully embraces the non-Western world.

Towards the end of his life, Francophone Africa received another benefit of John Stott's ministry, through his concern to develop expository preaching. Over the last few years, Langham Preaching seminars have been held in several countries including Côte d'Ivoire, Benin and Burkina Faso.

John Stott was also a remarkably faithful friend. He valued people and encouraged them in their faith. He never forgot me after our first meeting, and he prayed for me. In 1999, knowing I was a biologist, he inscribed a copy of his book *The Birds Our Teachers* and sent it to me in Abidjan, Côte d'Ivoire.

When I was called to my current role as General Secretary of IFES, Uncle John invited me to visit him, with Lindsay Brown, from whom I was taking over. At that time, in the summer of 2007, Uncle John was recovering from a fall and confined to bed, but he received us with great enthusiasm. He gave me several pieces of advice, one of which was the need to affirm the uniqueness of Jesus in a pluralist world. He prayed

## HE RECEIVED US WITH GREAT ENTHUSIASM

for me and for the ministry of IFES. It was a very significant moment for me, to be sent out with the prayer of this elder brother, model and mentor. I was still waiting to move with my family from Abidjan to Oxford, to take up my new role, and Uncle John lent help by writing to the British government, to request that they grant me the needed permissions.

Uncle John's parish extended to Francophone Africa. We give thanks to God for his life of service and his humility which always pointed people to the cross of Jesus.

*Dr Daniel Bourdanné, former General Secretary of IFES (2007-2019), served earlier as IFES Regional Secretary for Francophone Africa. He is a former International Deputy Director and former Board member of the Lausanne Movement.*

# 'WHAT I LEARNED FROM UNCLE JOHN STOTT'

### Femi Adeleye

I first heard of the Revd Dr John Stott while I was a student in Ahmadu Bello University, in Zaria, Nigeria, in the 1970s. We first met in Chicago in 1986, when I was studying at Wheaton Graduate School, and from those days I began to know him as a friend. He was deeply committed to nurturing a younger generation of leaders for the church, particularly in the non-Western world. For many of us in Africa, Uncle John was first a friend and then a mentor. My story is not unique; Uncle John gave generously of himself to those he got to know. Let me share three things I learnt from him.

> UNCLE JOHN WAS FIRST A FRIEND AND THEN A MENTOR

*First*: From before I met him, Uncle John taught me that my mind matters. I began student ministry with NIFES in 1980 as a young graduate, armed with what I had learnt in the Christian fellowship on campus, and my sociology degree. Soon afterwards I read Uncle John's book *Your Mind Matters*. It changed my attitude and disposition towards biblical scholarship; up to then I felt all that mattered was the Holy Spirit. Uncle John taught me that using my mind was as important as walking in, and working with, the Holy Spirit.

With his encouragement, I have studied Christian history and theology. He suggested I pursue a doctorate at Aberdeen University, after I finished at Wheaton Graduate School. The very same week that I received the offer of a Langham Scholarship, I also received an invitation to return to Nigeria to serve as NIFES General Secretary. What a dilemma to choose. Uncle John encouraged me to follow my conviction; he promised that the scholarship would be kept open, should I decide to serve in NIFES first. I

*UNCLE JOHN ENCOURAGED ME TO FOLLOW MY CONVICTION*

returned to Nigeria, and served in NIFES before later studying for a Masters in Theology at the University of Edinburgh. To congratulate me on completing my Masters, Uncle John sent me a copy of *Birds of West Africa*. More recently, by God's grace, I have once more been a beneficiary of a Langham scholarship, this time for a doctorate in African Christian history, from the Akrofi-Christaller Institute of Theology in Ghana.

*Secondly*: Uncle John was clearly concerned about issues facing the church on the African continent. In 1999 Bishop David Zac Niringiye and I started the Institute of Christian Impact for IFES in English- and Portuguese-speaking Africa.[96] Uncle John delivered the inaugural address in Kampala. He also gave a public lecture, attended by most members of the

---

96. David Zac Niringyie, former Assistant Bishop of Kampala, was at that time IFES Regional Secretary for English- and Portuguese-speaking Africa.

Ugandan House of Parliament. He challenged us to be bold in our Christian witness in the public arena. In addition, he has empowered the church in Africa through the threefold ministry

## HE CHALLENGED US TO BE BOLD IN THE PUBLIC ARENA

of Langham Partnership.[97] Through his own books he has left us a library to help us engage with issues in the church and in society.

*Thirdly*: Uncle John's life taught me humility. When I visited him in his pad for tea, after preaching at All Souls in February 2006, I was struck with the depth of his humility. We talked over aspects of life and ministry, then he asked me to pray for him, and without the slightest hesitation, now aged 84, he went on his knees. As we knelt and prayed together, I was overwhelmed by both his humility, and his intimacy with God.

The opportunity to know and interact with Uncle John has had significant impact on my life and ministry: within Nigeria, across Africa, and around the world. I will never be an Uncle John, but I can in my own way emulate the values I learnt from him.

*Dr Femi B Adeleye served for over 30 years with IFES in leadership at national, regional and global levels. Femi was a plenary speaker at The Third Lausanne Congress. He is Director of Langham Preaching for Africa.*

---

97. See p31.

# JOHN STOTT: GOD'S GIFT TO THE CHURCH IN LATIN AMERICA

## Samuel Escobar

John Stott has left a deep mark on the Protestant communities of Latin America. There are good memories of his many visits from the first in 1974 (Mexico, Perú, Chile and Argentina) to the last in 2001 (Lima, Perú). *Basic Christianity* appeared in Spanish in 1959, and by the time he died twenty-six of his books had been translated and published in Spanish, and a good number in Portuguese; some reprinted several times. He was equally appreciated among Pentecostals and Presbyterians, among Baptists and Methodists, and among Lutherans and the vast number of independent churches that make up the growing Protestant people in this part of the world.

Let me start with student work, my own sphere of ministry for 26 years all over Latin America. *Basic Christianity* was an excellent tool – for communicating the gospel at university level, and for deepening the understanding of students who had committed their lives to Christ. During John Stott's visits, we usually tried to get senior student leaders to his Bible expositions and seminars. He was very good in dialogues that

followed, and very precise in answers to questions.
He also participated in, and enjoyed, celebrations,
so students felt he was close to them. Several
generations found the Spanish
version of *Your Mind Matters* a
liberating experience, because
fundamentalist missionaries
had left behind a kind of anti-

> **STUDENTS FELT HE WAS CLOSE TO THEM**

intellectual bias. René Padilla got the best translator in
the publishing community to translate it in 1974.

We were committed to making Bible exposition
central in our training programs. We wanted growing
churches to be able to enjoy it and practise it. Stott's
exposition did not lose its force in translation. I have
in my memory the picture of Peruvian, Argentinian and
Mexican students absorbed as they listened, and at the
end exclaiming, 'That is the kind of preacher I want to be!'

In 1969 we held the First Latin American Congress
of Evangelism in Bogotá, Colombia. Here a group of
evangelists, pastors, seminary faculty, and lay leaders
decided to found a fellowship to encourage theological
reflection which was both evangelical and relevant
to our context. The following year the Latin American
Theological Fraternity (FTL) was founded. Some of its
members (such as René Padilla, Orlando Costas, Peter
Savage, Emilio Antonio Núñez and I) were speakers at
the 1974 Lausanne Congress on World Evangelization.
John Stott chaired the drafting committee for *The
Lausanne Covenant*. We knew this guaranteed that

voices from the Majority World would be heard. His global ministry was making him sensitive to the concerns of a new generation of evangelical leaders, and to the traditional paternalism of the West. Over the decades that followed, Stott modeled servant-leadership in the Lausanne Movement.

During his visits to Latin America (several of them coordinated by the FTL or the evangelical student movements), we would intentionally invite pastors and missionaries who were not related to these bodies, because his model of Bible exposition was greatly needed in our churches. When the FTL was founded in 1970, its *Cochabamba Declaration* stated: 'Preaching is often void of biblical substance. The evangelical pulpit is in a state of crisis. We find among ourselves a depressing ignorance of the Bible and of the application of its message to today's needs. The biblical message is indisputably pertinent to Latin Americans, but its proclamation does not play the part it should among us.'[98] We were committed to changing this.

Stott supported us in this effort and always encouraged us. There is now a new generation of Bible expositors, who, in one way or other, were schooled under Stott's ministry.[99] Angelit Guzmán was with him in

---

98. See complete text in *Latin American Evangelical Theology in the 1970's*, Ed: Daniel Salinas (Brill, 2009) pp 200-201.

99. For example Valdir Steuernagel and Ziel Machado (Brazilians), Jorge Atiencia (Ecuadorian), Darío López and Angelit Guzmán (Peruvian) and Carmen Pérez de Camargo (Mexican) and others.

Cuba in 1996 and she took some of his expositions and edited them for publication with pieces written by Jorge Atiencia and myself under the title *Así leo la Biblia*.[100] We wrote about applying the Bible in our lives, and how to prepare Bible expositions. Now expositors from several generations have made contributions to the one volume *Latin American Bible Commentary*.[101]

His status as an Anglican minister active in his church has been of help to Latin American evangelicals who had a strong anti-Roman Catholic bias, coming from their evangelical convictions and from their experience as a persecuted religious minority in Latin America. His personal stance as an evangelical taking part in the Evangelical-Roman Catholic Dialogue on Mission was an eye-opener to many; some were at first shocked or surprised by his participation. The Report he co-edited with Monsignor Basil Meeking shows his openness to dialogue, his recognition of a wide common ground and at the same time his firmness in convictions from which he would not yield an inch.[102] Among evangelicals in Latin America and southern Europe there is still a long way to go in terms of defining a mature attitude in relation to

---

100. *This is the way I read the Bible*. Contributors: Jorge Atiencia, Samuel Escobar, John Stott. *Así leo la Biblia*, (Certeza Unida, 1999).

101. Edited by René Padilla (Argentina), Rosalee Velloso (Brazil) and Milton Acosta (Colombia). Published with the help of Langham Partnership, 2012.

102. *The Evangelical-Roman Catholic dialogue on Mission*. Published in Spanish the same year.

Roman Catholicism and issues of ecumenism. I think that Stott's ecclesiology, if adequately identified and expounded, could be a great help.

Stott's commitment to an evangelicalism that is faithful to its basic convictions, but not sectarian or narrow-minded, was a great gift to the church universal during the second part of the twentieth century. His ability to mediate creatively between positions that were sometimes exaggerated or intolerant required a good measure of patience, openness and self-control as well as a good

*HIS ABILITY TO MEDIATE REQUIRED PATIENCE, OPENNESS AND SELF-CONTROL*

command of words. These gifts were evident in his contributions to the Lausanne Movement. The depth, quality and clarity of documents such as The Lausanne Covenant (1974), the Willowbank Report on Gospel and Culture (1978) or the Grand Rapids Report on Gospel and Social Responsibility (1982) owe much to his hard work as both a chair person and a writer.[103] We Latin Americans have added the cultural and national biases of our own background to the divisiveness received from the European or North American missionary heritage. So the evangelical enterprise is far from being an easy road to walk. For those of us that worked with Stott in global projects, his example was a great

---

103. Collected in *Making Christ Known*.

blessing and inspiration, as well as a model we tried to follow.

Through these years I have also witnessed the role of John Stott as an encourager. In some gatherings were missionaries or pastors who faced critical situations. Stott always offered an attentive ear. His emphasis on a missionary lifestyle modeled after the pattern of Jesus could have been difficult for some to hear. But he knew how to offer clear teaching from the front about Christ's demands, while also offering personal counsel in private conversation. For me, it was only through his continual encouragement that I adopted the discipline of setting apart time for writing, just as I took specific time for speaking engagements.[104]

In conversation, one could perceive how much John Stott had changed as a result of his international trips, and his encounters with other cultures and other parts of the church. As I think back to the drafting of *The Lausanne Covenant*, I remember the moment he coined the final sentence of paragraph 10: 'Christ's evangelists must humbly seek to empty themselves of all but their personal authenticity in order to become the servants of others, and churches must seek to transform and enrich culture, all for the glory of God.' What rich, careful, and perceptive words.

---

104. My book *A Time for Mission* (2003, USA title The New Global Mission) in the Global Christian Library came as a result of much patient and systematic encouragement from John Stott and David Smith.

You can listen to John Stott's presentation of *The Lausanne Covenant* on the last full day of the 1974 Congress at *lausanne.org*. He and his drafting team of Hudson Armerding and myself, assisted by J D Douglas and Leighton Ford, invited comments at each stage of the process. We received hundreds, which were all translated and carefully considered. It was a finely-tuned and meticulous process. The *Covenant* truly reflected the mood of the Lausanne Congress as well as any single document could.

When he came to minister in Latin America, he did his best to put into practice that Christlike form of ministry. He did not come across as the typical British gentleman. He left behind some attitudes of class and nationality, and learned much along the way, not only in terms of food, simple lifestyle, or *siesta* time, but also in terms of theology. This is evident, for instance, in the second part of his book *The Incomparable Christ* (2001). And that is another reason why his books will continue being enjoyed, and transforming lives, in Latin America.

*HE DID NOT COME ACROSS AS THE TYPICAL BRITISH GENTLEMAN*

*Prof Samuel Escobar, from Peru, widely-known writer and missiologist, was a speaker at Lausanne 1974. After 26 years with IFES in Latin America, he taught at Palmer Theological Seminary, Philadelphia. He has now retired to Valencia, Spain.*

# PART V

# FAREWELL WORDS

Uncle John: 'An uncle with a grandfather's face'. (See p120.)

# POEMA

**Eidi Cruz-Valdivieso**

This poem was forwarded to the Editor by Frances Whitehead at the end of November 2011, when the first edition of this book was already in the late stage of design. The unique perspective the poem brought on Uncle John ('an uncle with a grandfather's face') was arresting, and it clearly needed to be included.

Eidi was with Frances, and members of John Stott's close family, when he died in the College of St Barnabas on 27 July 2011. She wrote her poem in Spanish, and then translated it into English.

Eidi writes:

> Uncle John was a profound influence on my family, and a lifetime friend. My Dad first met him in Mexico, when still a young teenager. He visited Armonía, my family's ministry amongst poor communities, and I remember his interest in seeing us children learning to serve others.

> I have memories from childhood of visiting the UK, and seeing him teach at LICC; of watching his beloved birds with him, and of imitating them flying – whilst he and my parents and Frances sat around The Hookses dining table!

Uncle John continued to be caring and deeply insightful even in the midst of his physical dimming. I treasure the many conversations we had, especially in his later years. He was a wonderfully wise, loving, and witty grandfather-figure in my life. Above all, he showed who Jesus was and is.

[For the English translation, see p119]

### El Tío Juan

El Tío Juan, con sus ojos pequeños,
llenos de inteligencia y de esperanza,
me enseñó.

Me enseñó de la disciplina,
que se nutre de ella misma.
Y de la simplicidad,
que se encuentra con la sabiduría,
caminando juntas
en obediencia;
admirando la complejidad de la Fe.

Me enseñó de Jesús,
quien es un Rey
vestido de arapos,
que camina con peces;
se sumerge en la oscuridad de nuestra indiferencia,
sangra y vuela hacia su muerte,
y regresa corriendo para decirme que todo va a estar bien.
Para siempre.

Me enseñó de la inteligencia,
que no lo intenta saber todo,
que empuja su propia vanidad
hasta no ver su reflejo.

Me enseñó del amor a la belleza de los pobres,
a la belleza de los pájaros,
a la belleza del trabajo,
a la belleza del misterio de Dios.

Me enseñó de la asertividad,
que es clara,
ante lo turbio de la hipocresía.
Que es valiente,
ante la sutileza de la manipulación.

Me enseñó de la humildad,
que usa su corona para adornar a otros.
Que ve a los niños como maestros,
que escucha a los demás
con la devoción con la que alguien escucha a un
    ruiseñor.

Y se fué.
Ese señor de ojos pequeños.
Ese hijo amado de Dios.
Ese hermano amado de tantos.
Ese Tío que me veía con cara de abuelo.
Con sus manitas que le temblaban tanto,

con su espalda que le dolía tanto,
con sus bromas que traían sol entre tanta lluvia,
con sus últimas palabras de amor a mi familia,
con los últimos destellos de genialidad en sus ojos,
con su compasión y su generosidad,
con una Fé profunda como concebimos al mar.

Y lo volveremos a ver,
volveremos a platicar,
nos volveremos a reír.
Pero esta vez sin lluvia.

*Eidi Cruz-Valdivieso*
*November, 2011*

Eidi's English translation of her poem.

## Uncle John

Uncle John, with his small eyes,
full of intelligence and hope,
taught me.

He taught me about discipline
that nurtures itself,
and about simplicity
that meets wisdom,
and walks together with her
in obedience
before the mystery of faith.

He taught me about Jesus,
who is a King,
dressed in rags.
Who walks with fish,
immerses himself in the darkness of our indifference,
bleeds and flies to his death,
and comes back running to tell me that everything will
     be fine.
Forever.

He taught me about intelligence
that doesn't try to know everything,

that pushes her own vanity away,
until its reflection can no longer be seen.


He taught me about loving the beauty of the poor,
the beauty of birds,
the beauty of work,
the beauty of the mystery of God.


He taught me about assertiveness
that is clear
as it faces the muddiness of hypocrisy.
Assertiveness that is courageous
when facing the subtle ways of manipulation.


He taught me about humility
that uses her crown to adorn others,
that sees children as teachers,
that listens to others
with the devotion with which we listen to a nightingale.


And he left.
That man of small eyes.
That beloved child of God.
That beloved brother to so many.
That Uncle who looked at me with a grandfather's face.


With his dear hands that were shaking so much,
with his back that hurt so much,

with his wittiness that brought sunshine in the midst of
    so much rain,
with the last words of love for my family,
with the last sparkle of genius in his eyes,
with his compassion and generosity,
with a faith as profound as the depths of the sea.

And we will see him again,
we will enjoy talking again,
we will laugh together again.
But this time there will be no rain.

*Eidi Cruz-Valdivieso*
*November, 2011*

### An 'au revoir' occasion

'The glorious, transcendent, reality of eternal life wonderfully eases the very real sense of loss we feel, that a Christian giant, a hero, a role model, a teacher, a mentor, an irreplaceable friend we loved – has gone. This is, however, supremely an au revoir occasion and you do not need firsts in French and Theology from Cambridge to know what that means!'

*His Honour, Judge David Turner at John Stott's funeral.*

### Finishing the race

'I have fought the good fight, I have finished the race, I have kept the faith. Now there is in store for me the crown of righteousness, which the Lord, the righteous Judge, will award to me on that day – and not only to me, but also to all who have longed for his appearing.' (2 Timothy 4:7-8)

'Those who are wise will shine like the brightness of the heavens, and those who lead many to righteousness like the stars, for ever and ever.' (Daniel 12:3)

# APPENDIX

## Books written by John Stott

We show the date of first publication only. Several titles were taken over by other publishers for later editions. Almost all are still in print, some having changed their title to cross the Atlantic, or to fit better into a new publisher's list.[105] NB This list does not include works edited.[106]

*Men with a Message* (Longmans, Green and Co, 1954)

*Basic Christianity* (IVP, 1958)

*Your Confirmation* (Hodder, 1958)

*What Christ thinks of the Church: Expository addresses on the first three chapters of the Book of Revelation* (Lutterworth, 1958)

*The Preacher's Portrait: Some New Testament word studies* (Tyndale, 1961)

*The Epistles of John: An Introduction and Commentary* (Tyndale, 1964)

*The Baptism and Fullness of the Holy Spirit* (IVF, 1964)

---

105. Each book was written in longhand, and from *Basic Christianity* onwards, all were typed by Frances Whitehead, amid her many responsibilities.

106. For this see *John Stott: A Comprehensive Bibliography* by Timothy Dudley-Smith (IVP UK, 1995; IVP US, 1996).

*The Canticles and Selected Psalms* (Hodder, 1966)

*Men Made New: An exposition of Romans 5-8* (IVP-UK; IVP-US, both 1966)

*Our Guilty Silence: The Church, the Gospel and the World* (EFAC with Hodder 1967)

*One People: Clergy and Laity in God's Church* (Falcon, 1969)

*Christ the Controversialist: A study in some essentials of evangelical religion* (Tyndale; IVP-UK, both 1970)

*Understanding the Bible* (Scripture Union and Gospel Light, 1972)

*Your Mind Matters: The place of the mind in the Christian life* (IVP-UK; IVP-US, both 1972)

*Balanced Christianity: A call to avoid unnecessary polarisation* (Hodder / IVP, 1975)

*Christian Mission in the Modern World* (Falcon / IVP, 1975)

*The Lausanne Covenant: An exposition and Commentary* (Worldwide Publications, USA, 1975) and as *Explaining the Lausanne Covenant* (Scripture Union, UK, 1975)

*Focus on Christ: An enquiry into the Theology of Presuppositions* (Collins UK and USA, both 1979)

*The Bible: Book for Today* (IVP-UK and IVP-US, both 1982)

*I Believe in Preaching* (Hodder and Eerdmans, both 1982). US title: *Between Two Worlds: The art of Preaching in the Twentieth Century*

*Issues Facing Christians Today* (Marshalls, 1984)

*The Authentic Jesus: A response to current scepticism in the Church* (Marshalls and IVP-US, both 1985)

*The Whole Christian* (IVP, Korea,1986)

*The Cross of Christ* (IVP-UK and IVP-US, both 1986)

*Essentials: A liberal-evangelical dialogue* (co-author David L Edwards. Hodder, 1988)

*The Lordship of Christ in South Africa* (Lectures given in major cities; published by Africa Enterprise, Pietermaritzburg. Some lectures formed part of the text in *The Contemporary Christian*)

*The Contemporary Christian: An urgent plea for double listening* (IVP-UK and IVP-US, both 1992)

*Problems of Christian Leadership* (translated into Spanish as *Desafíos del liderazgo*. Certeza Argentina, Buenos Aires, 1992 and as *Los Problemas del Liderazgo Cristiano*, Ediciones PUMA, Lima / AGUEP, Lima, 1994)

*People called to be Different* (Published in Spanish as *Llamados a ser diferentes*. IINDEF, Costa Rica, 1998)

*Evangelical Truth: A personal plea for unity* (IVP-UK and IVP-US, both 1999). In US subtitled: *A personal plea for Unity, Integrity and Faithfulness*.

*The Birds our Teachers: Biblical lessons from a lifelong birdwatcher* (Also subtitled *Essays in Orni-theology*) (Candle Books, 1999)

*The Incomparable Christ*: Based on the AD 2000 London Lectures in Contemporary Christianity (IVP-UK and IVP-US, both 2001)

*Calling Christian Leaders: Biblical models of church, gospel and ministry* (IVP-UK, 2002) In US subtitled *Basic Christian leadership* (IVP-US, also 2002)

*People my Teachers: Around the world in eighty years* (Candle Books, 2002)

*The Church in the New Millennium: Three studies in the Acts of the Apostles* (Zapf Chancery, Eldoret, Kenya, 2002)

*Why I am a Christian: This is my story* (IVP-UK and IVP-US, both 2003)

*Through the Bible Through the Year: daily reflections from Genesis to Revelation* (Candle Books, UK and Baker Books, USA. Both 2006)

*The Living Church: Convictions of a Lifelong Pastor* (IVP-UK and IVP-US, both 2007)

*The Last Word: Reflections on a Lifetime of Preaching*. Keswick address, 2007. (Keswick Classics, Authentic Media UK, US and India, all 2008)

*John Stott at Keswick: A lifetime of preaching*. Keswick addresses. (Keswick Classics, Authentic Media UK, US and India, all 2008)

*The Radical Disciple: Wholehearted Christian Living* (IVP-UK; IVP-US, both 2010). In US subtitled: *Some Neglected aspects of our Calling.*

*Students of the Word: Engaging with Scripture to impact our world.* Addresses given to IFES Graduates Conference, 2006. (IFES, 2013)

**The Bible Speaks Today series** (All IVP, UK and USA)

*The Message of Galatians* (1968) Subtitled *Only One Way*

*The Message of 2 Timothy* (1973) Subtitled *Guard the Gospel*

*The Message of the Sermon on the Mount* (1978) Subtitled *Christian Counter-Culture*

*The Message of Ephesians* (1979) Subtitled *God's New Society*

*The Message of Acts* (UK 1990) *Subtitled To the Ends of the Earth*; Published in US as *The Spirit, the Church and the World* (1990)

*The Message of Thessalonians* (1991) Subtitled *Preparing for the Coming King.* Published in US as *The Gospel and the End of Time* (1991)

*The Message of Romans* (UK, 1994) Subtitled *God's Good News for the World.* Published in US as *Romans: God's Good News for the World* (also 1994)

*The Message of 1 Timothy and Titus* (UK, 1996). Subtitled *The Life of the Local Church.* Published in US as *Guard the Truth* (also 1996)

## SELECTED FURTHER READING

### Biographical

*John Stott: The Early Years* and *John Stott: The Making of a Leader*. Classic two-volume authorized biography by Timothy Dudley-Smith. Superbly indexed. (IVP, 1999 and 2001)

*John Stott: A Portrait by his Friends*, Ed Chris Wright. *Festschrift* for 90th birthday. (IVP, 2011)

*John Stott's Right Hand: The untold story of Frances Whitehead*. Brings a unique angle on John Stott's life and ministry. Authorized biography by Julia Cameron. (Piquant, 2014. Expanded and updated edition, Dictum / EFAC, 2020)

### For children

*John Stott: Call me 'Uncle John'* by Julia Cameron. Fun authorized biography written for children. Features a timeline, maps and 25 'Fascinating Facts'. (Dictum / EFAC, 2021)

### Also recommended

*The Birds our Teachers* by John Stott. Full of spiritual lessons. (Candle / Hendrickson, 1999)

*Charles Simeon of Cambridge: Silhouettes and Skeletons*, Ed J E M Cameron. Charles Simeon (1759-1836) was John Stott's mentor, through his writing. (Revised edition, Wipf and Stock, 2019)

EFAC Global was founded in 1961 by John Stott as the Evangelical Fellowship in the Anglican Communion. Its role has become even more critical in recent years.

Through local fellowships, EFAC serves to encourage and develop biblical literacy, vital to healthy doctrine and practice, and effective mission, to build *'Bible People. Gospel People. Church People.'* EFAC works to equip leaders to stand firm, to engage thoughtfully with secular trends, and to articulate a persuasive biblical response. Its affiliated group in the UK is the Church of England Evangelical Council.

EFAC's Theology Resource Network (TRN) draws senior theologians from all continents. As John Stott was always keen to remind EFAC's early members, Christ gave gifts to his church to share. Through the TRN's international membership, insights from many contexts are shared around the table, and then shared more widely through gatherings and in print.

Christ prayed in Gethsemane for the future church to be unified; 'at one' with its Apostolic roots (John 17:20ff). EFAC, under the leadership of an International Council and General Secretary, and through its Theology Resource Network, local fellowships and small team, seeks to further true unity.

To learn more, visit *efacglobal.com*

Clarity and brevity are two great gifts to the world. *Dictum's* short books do not waste words, or waste the reader's time. They bring biblical thinking which is refreshing, clear, and well-applied. Our values are summed up as 'Biblical. Pastoral. Incisive.'

To serve the UK church and mission agencies, *Dictum* publishes a handful of core titles, all modern classics, offering them at bulk discount. (A review copy may be ordered at no charge.) Books include questions for discussion in a group context, or for personal reflection.

Our list is not long, and our titles include classic reprints. We focus on sourcing some of the best evangelical writing available.

Further, in collaboration with Day One, *Dictum* publishes the *Oxford and Cambridge Reformation Walking Tour*, a self-guided tour taking 90 minutes in each university town. This will be of interest to anyone who values Reformation history, whether or not they can visit these locations.

Agencies or churches ordering in bulk are invited to feature their logo, and a description of their ministry, at the front of titles purchased.

*Dictum* is pleased to work with EFAC Global in a partnership which maximises the reach of books.

For more visit *dictumpress.com*

# ALSO IN THIS SERIES

*The Cross: A fresh look at the meaning of the death of Christ* by James Philip

*Money and the Gospel: Giving money with grace and Handling money with integrity* by John Stott and Chris Wright

*Take Care of Yourself: How to survive and thrive in Christian ministry* by Pablo Martinez

*The Leadership Files: From around the world, across a century* Vaughan Roberts, Ajith Fernando, John Stott et al.

*The Authority of the Bible* by John Stott. Includes the widely-used McCheyne Reading Plan

*Oxford and Cambridge Reformation Walking Tour* by Julia E M Cameron

For a growing list of titles, visit *dictumpress.com*